FROM
FUN
To
Fortune

FROM FUN To Fortune

The traumatic birth and growth of professional sports in America's phantom city

By Pete Geissler

2024 by Pete Geissler

All rights reserved. No part of this publication may be reproduced, distributed, or transmitted in any form or by any means, including photocopying, recording, or other electronic or mechanical methods, without the prior written permission of the publisher, except in the case of brief quotations embodied in critical reviews and certain other noncommercial uses permitted by copyright law. For permission requests, write to The Expressive Press. expressivepress@gmail.com

All photographs are public domain images sourced from the Library of Congress and the New York Public Library.

First edition October 2024

Design by Darren Geissler

ISBN: 979-8-3304-7302-1

Published by The Expressive Press

www.TheExpressivePress.org

FROM FUN To Fortune

The traumatic birth and growth of professional sports in America's phantom city

By Pete Geissler

2024 by Pete Geissler

All rights reserved. No part of this publication may be reproduced, distributed, or transmitted in any form or by any means, including photocopying, recording, or other electronic or mechanical methods, without the prior written permission of the publisher, except in the case of brief quotations embodied in critical reviews and certain other noncommercial uses permitted by copyright law. For permission requests, write to The Expressive Press. expressivepress@gmail.com

All photographs are public domain images sourced from the Library of Congress and the New York Public Library.

First edition October 2024

Design by Darren Geissler

ISBN: 979-8-3304-7302-1

Published by The Expressive Press

www.TheExpressivePress.org

The Savants Sound Off About Fun To Fortune

"Pete Geissler has shown once again that he is the master of narrating history disguised as a biting, bare-knuckle novel with real and imagined characters and settings. My bucket list is topped with meeting Sarah Scrivener, the crusading journalist and protagonist in this wonderful mind-bender."

Susan Tusick, CEO, Tusick & Associates Architects

"A delightful combination of fact, fiction, opinion, and imagination that will jump start your heart and challenge your mind with many enlightening moments. A wonderful read and future movie or TV series by a gifted writer."

Barry Wolfe, author of the globally popular *The Little Black Book of HR Management*

"Pete Geissler has taken the gloves off to write this cheeky, fast-paced speculative drama that entertains, enlightens, and engages sports fans, fun seekers, and history buffs of all ages and persuasions."

Ken Lovorn, BSEE, President and Owner, Lovorn Engineering

"If you've ever pondered how and why humans worldwide became so enamored with sports, ponder no more. Geissler has given us the reasons."

Joe Sinnott, MSCE, Career Coach for the upwardly mobile

CONTENTS

1. The Back Story   8
- The Ultimate Team
- Meet Sarah Scrivener
- Thank you, Abe Lincoln

2. Birthing Modern Football   28
- Joseph Siebeneck introduces Sarah
- Allegheny Athletic Association
- First official football game
- The first professionals
- Walter Camp

3. Birthing Modern Baseball   65
- Who invented baseball?
- The leagues emerge
- AAA's MVPs
- The dignitaries behind the curtains
- The first world series?

4. Is there a future for organized sports?   96
- Stop abusing umpires
- A code of ethics

5. Epilogue   104
- Sarah speaks at the Western University of Pittsburgh

6. Appendices   109
1. America in the Gilded Age
2. The Author and FUN
3. Early Sports Lore
4. Neilie Bly, Celebrating Allegheny City
5. The Jargon of Sports in The 19th Century
6. Other books by Pete Geissler

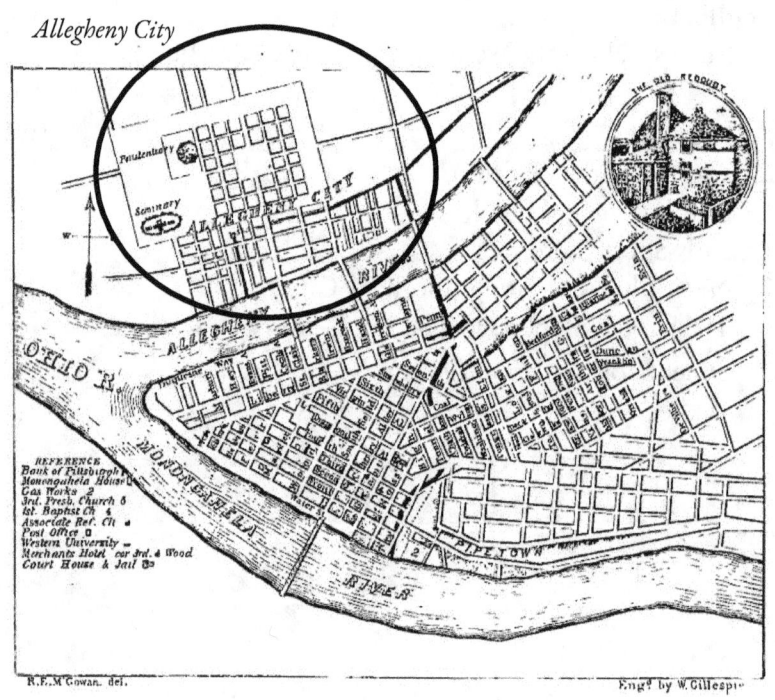

1.

THE BACK STORY:

The Ultimate Team: America, Allegheny City, And Sports

The birth and growth of America, Allegheny City, and organized sports are laced so tightly as to be one.

Modern America is the social/political/economic experiment that became the most powerful economy and military in history. It was created by a handful of visionaries and entrepreneurs–our Founding Fathers—willing to risk their lives, fortunes, and reputations for untold wealth and lasting fame. It was perpetuated by our tycoons and entrepreneurs with similar appetites for risk, fame, and fortune. Among them were Andrew Carnegie, George Westinghouse, and George Ferris, all of whom lived for an abbreviated time in Allegheny City, the city that began in wilderness, evolved in prosperity, and died in political ambition. It is a city without a map or identity. It is The Phantom City.

Modern sports were laced tightly with Modern America by a handful of adventurers, many of whom were accomplished athletes as well. They played for the love of the game and then for pay that was not enough to support a thankless, sparse life, so most worked a second job. They were the early professional and freelance athletes confronted with new careers in a newly prosperous America that embraced them. Should we thank or curse them for manipulating our lives?

Early professional athletes could not have known at the time— the mid-1800s to 1920 and beyond—that they helped to spawn the Age of Mass Organized Sports and its hysterics, instant millionaires, and excesses that often stretched the bounds of legality and ethics.

The times were part of The Gilded Age, The Age of Iron, Steel and Steam, of Unbounded Optimism, of The Gay Nineties, of

Consumerism spurred by a plethora of new products that enhanced the quality of life for those who could afford them. It was a time of riotous economic growth that naive optimists knew would never end. Realists knew better.

It positioned America as the richest, most productive, most powerful, most fanatical nation on the planet. It positioned America to be the upstart cradle of prosperity for many and sports for all.

*

Not all Americans were on this gilded, deceptive path. Many coal miners and steelworkers, for example, were discouraged and sullen. They toiled for wages that were barely able to sustain a decent life. The wages were dictated by owners and entrepreneurs, many of whom were more interested in profits than workers' welfare. Workers toiled long hours in hot, dangerous mines and mills, lived in company houses and towns that were squalid and ugly. They were forced by circumstances to breathe air and drink water polluted by poisonous discharges that led to deadly diseases such as tuberculosis, black lung, and stomach ulcers. Other unskilled workers suffered similar fates.

*

Caveat:

FUN is not a history text. It is a speculative drama, aka historical fiction, which is a creative mixture of verifiable historical events and characters, imagined conversations, and thoughtful opinion presented in lively and engaging prose. It breathes fresh life into history while it shatters some long-held beliefs that have become myths rivaling Santa Claus and The Easter Bunny. No question that myths surround the realities of Abner Doubleday, Pudge Heffelfinger, the first World Series, The Ferris Wheel, The Columbian EXPO, George Westinghouse, and many others of the day.

All *FUN* players are real except Sarah Scrivener, your host, narrator, and journalist with a flair for drama and unblemished prose that demands readers' attention and admiration. She is imagined by the author.

FUN is, however, the author's fourth cheeky, fast-paced, fact-based speculative drama; like the others, it is guaranteed to entertain, enlighten, and engage curious sports fans, fun seekers, and history buffs of all ages and persuasions. Enjoy.

More about The Phantom City:

Allegheny City was founded in 1787 as a reserve land tract that was parceled out to veterans of The Revolutionary War to reward them for their service. It soon evolved into its own thriving community that attracted a variety of residents with diverse talents and interests. Among them were steel billionaire and philanthropist Andrew Carnegie whose 3500 community libraries dot America; engineer George Ferris whose wheels poke into the sky around the world is in The Engineers' Hall of Fame at Rensselaer Polytechnical Institute, his prestigious alma mater; impressionist artist Mary Cassatt who partied in Paris with Van Gogh, Claude Monet, and Toulouse Lautrec; author Gertrude Stein who is famed for reminding us that a rose is a rose by any other name and smells as sweet; and composer Stephen Foster, who wrote endearing folk songs that are a permanent slice of our culture.

The abutting City of Pittsburgh annexed the area in 1907 after a bitter political fight. It is now known as Pittsburgh's North Side or North Shore.

In the mid to late 1800s-early 1900s Allegheny City was a magnet for sports, with Exposition and Recreation Parks, both of which hosted baseball and football games and neighborhood fairs and circuses. Now, in the mid-twenty-first century, The North Side hosts two major arenas: PNC Park (formerly Three Rivers Stadium) for the Pittsburgh Pirates and some impressive wine tastings, and Acrisure Stadium (formerly Heinz Field) to host the Pittsburgh Steelers, University of Pittsburgh Panthers football games, championship games played by several regional high schools, and concerts by major entertainers.

PNC Park, Pittsburgh

History infuses the area and is preserved by prominent markers (including the site of Franco Hariss's Immaculate Reception) and bigger-than-life bronze statues of sports heroes such as Pirates Honus Wagner, Roberto Clemente, Bill Mazeroski, and Willy Stargell.

Residents enjoyed an active social life in several local pubs and hotels. One of the more popular and active was The Farmers & Drovers Hotel on Suisman Street. George Rahn, a successful saloon owner, purchased and combined two historic hotels in 1900 and, in 1903 (just in time for the first world series played only a half mile away) built the Hotel Rahn on the corner lot next door. It is now the main bar and dining room of Max's Allegheny Tavern, a popular meeting spot that features German beer and fare. A few years later—say 1905, 1906—Rahn bought the beautiful hand-carved wooden bar from the St. Louis Exposition (noted for the first hamburgers, ice cream

Max's Allegheny Tavern, early 1900s

cones, and iced tea among other goodies in 1904) and installed it in The Tavern. It also features a patterned, ceramic tile floor, etched glass windows, tin ceilings, upright player piano, and vintage wooden ice boxes bulging with beer and wine.

Also in 1903, Tom Edison ordered his technicians to electrocute

13 | From Fun to Fortune

Topsy, an innocent circus elephant, to demonstrate that George Westinghouse's alternating current—AC—is more lethal than his direct current—DC. It didn't. But it did add fire to America's early Standards War—would we electrify the country with AC or DC current? The unfortunate and monumentally cruel incident took place, ironically, on Coney Island, the icon of pleasure.

Topsy, standing in the middle of press photographers and on-lookers, 1903.

Preamble: Setting The Stage: It all started with a speech

Sarah Scrivener introduces herself; America the Bountiful was—and remains—fertile ground for sports and wealth.

May 1886, the campus of Syracuse University

Good afternoon. My name is Sarah Scrivener, and I am honored to be your commencement speaker.

God has blessed us with a rare but welcome balmy day in this Spring of 1886, for our graduation celebrations. I am honored, as I am sure my fellow graduates of the School of Journalism are, to welcome the Governor of New York, the honorable David B. Hill. I wish him well as he manages the affairs of this great state. New York will surely prosper under his able leadership.

*

David Bennett Hill (August 29, 1843 – October 20, 1910) was the 29th governor of New York from 1885 to 1891, and United States Senator from New York from 1892 to 1897. In 1892, He lost his party's nomination for President of The United States to Grover Cleveland, his longtime political rival and former running mate. Cleveland went on to be the only President elected to two nonconsecutive terms: 1888-1891 and 1893-1897. In May 1893 he visited The Columbian EXPO in Chicago, a month before the maiden trip of

David Bennett Hill

the first Ferris Wheel and two months before the initial lawsuits were filed against George Ferris for patent infringement that would eventually ruin him. That summer, Americans were shocked to notice the first rumblings of a major economic depression.

I, Sarah Scrivener, confess. I confess that I am madly and irrevocably in love with journalism, an honorable profession populated by honorable men and a few women with the courage to plow new ground in a man's world. God willing, journalism will be my lifetime pursuit, and I am grateful that it started here. Yes, devoting the last four years to studying its ins and outs, its goods and bads, its pluses and minuses, has been among my greatest pleasures, along with getting to know and exchanging ideas with my classmates and professors. Thanks to all of you for traveling with me.

I have valid, strong reasons for loving journalism, and I'd wager that you share them with me.

First, it gives me license to witness the inside stories behind our government and other institutions and organizations. Governor Hill, I plan to interview you someday, perhaps as you are being sworn in as our country's president. I will be the fly on the wall, the man in the street, the reporter of your every word and deed. Look for me.

Second, journalism has given me an unwavering respect for truth and the need to deliver the truth to the public. I will provide new levels of objectivity and truth in my columns. I am driven and committed to find and report the truth wherever it might hide from my prying and curious eyes, and deliver it, unfiltered and unadulterated, to my readers. To you.

We learned here at the university that there is more than one truth about most events, that there are more than two sides to every story.

We journalists have the awesome power to select truths constructively to inspire and prod organizations and individuals to serve their constituents more efficiently, encourage children and others to live ethically with integrity, and drive beneficial change to our vibrant society. Or we can select truths that give false impressions of reality, misleading people without reverting to lies, also known as false or yellow news. It must be avoided.

*

Journalism lost its moral compass in the 1890s when it reverted to 'Yellow news'. Events were hyped and imagined during the circulation war between Joseph Pulitzers' New York World and William Randolph Hearst's New York Journal. The war, which became part of the movie Citizen Kane, *peaked between 1895 and 1898 and featured lurid headlines and fabricated stories; the more lurid and fabricated the better. Truth was ignored, and eye-catching, mind-bending pictures, headlines, and text were revered and rewarded. Perhaps truth made a comeback during the two world wars, the space race, and the cold war, but has lost its moral compass again with the infighting and biases of politics.*

*

In short, we journalists must always consider that our pen—even our collective pens—is mightier than our sword, and we must wield it wisely if our society will continue to grow and prosper. All of us here are well equipped to tackle that task with the honesty, integrity, and truth it deserves. . . and which we were taught here at this great university.

My best reason to love journalism is this: Being a journalist is one of the few professions open to women. Nellie Bly, the pseudonym for a female reporter working for The Pittsburgh Dispatch is in the process of proving that truth, and I will support and perpetuate it to the best of my energies and abilities. I have accepted a job as cub reporter with Joseph Pulitzer and his New York World, and hope to specialize in reporting America's enviable growth, and particularly its latest obsession, organized sports.

I see football and baseball, with a growing nod to basketball, tennis, harness racing, boxing, golf, swimming, and soccer, as the new opium for the masses. Sports will replace religion and beer, mark my words, as America becomes more industrialized, and our citizens earn more excess cash to spend on new, unimagined products and on performances such as the multitude of circuses that crawl our landscape .P.T. Barnum, The Ringling Brothers, James Bailey, and many smaller troupes such as Sparks' World Famous Shows and Circuses are competing with each other and with other forms of entertainment for our time and money.

Many citizens will spend more time and money on sports during more leisure time brought about by higher productivity and profits and less need for labor. It's all a beneficial spin off of industrialization, our recognition that people cannot work productively and profitably 70-80 hours per week when 40-50 would be more acceptable and humane. In short, industrialization accelerated the nation's transition from the farm to the city, from using our bodies to earn a living to using our minds.

    Sarah was more prophetic and insightful than she could have imagined. In 1897 Louis and Charles Clark started producing The Pittsburgher cars, eventually producing three thousand of them near Allegheny City. In 1900, R. E. Olds first assembled his Oldsmobiles from parts made by other manufacturers, unleashing the efficiencies of Mass Production and the assembly line. In 1903, Henry Ford organized The Ford Motor Company, which, in 1908, introduced its Model T. All these commercial pioneers helped initiate our love affair with cars and for the joys of greater mobility, the Sunday drive, and easier commute to jobs in factories and offices that were increasingly located outside city limits.

*

    I predict that we are on the edge of The Age of Information, Intelligence, and Engineering. If proof is needed, consider that the Erie Canal was completed in 1825, the transcontinental Railroad was completed in 1869, and the Brooklyn Bridge was completed in 1883, only three years ago. Being planned as we speak is the Columbian Exposition, the world's largest and most opulent construction project scheduled to open in 1892 to celebrate the 400th anniversary of Columbus' arrival in the Americas. You are well prepared to participate and benefit fully.

    Good luck to all as you make practical use of all that you have learned during the past four years. I sincerely hope that you and all humanity benefit with the prosperity and happiness that you deserve. Thank you, and I plan to see you all at our first reunion.

Only a few months later, Charles Martin Hall, working in Pittsburgh in a laboratory on Smallman Street just across The Allegheny River from Allegheny City, filed a patent for his inexpensive method for smelting bauxite to make aluminum, creating an entire new industry. At about the same time, Paul Hérault discovered the same process while working in France; it became known as the Hall- Hérault- Process.

Hall's and Hérault's ingenuity spurred the development and growth of many other industries, among them mining and oil, Glass, and automobiles. In and near Allegheny City George Westinghouse expanded his air brake company to include making many products to generate, transmit, and use electricity; Andrew Carnegie's steel company soon became the world's largest and most profitable; James Laughlin and his partner Benjamiin Jones formed J & L Steel to challenge Carnegie; George Mesta manufactured the huge mills that rolled, forged, and extruded raw steel into more useful shapes; H.J. Heinz was building in Allegheny City, one of the more productive food processing plants in the world; George Ferris formed his engineering company that designed the first Ferris Wheel …

These industries put people to work and attracted immigrants from the world over. Soon the workers, many in Allegheny City and Pittsburgh where jobs were plentiful, were earning a living wage, thanks in large part to their unions and collective bargaining. Workers eventually broke free from the back-breaking 12-hour day, seven days per week schedule that consumed their lives and well-being. Soon, workers had discretionary time and a small amount of money to spend on pleasures such as circuses and sports.

Elizabeth Jane Cochran (Nellie Bly) was an American journalist who wrote for The Pittsburgh Dispatch *and launched investigative reporting. She is most renowned for traveling around the world in a record-breaking seventy-two days, breaking Phineas Fogg's record of eighty days in Jules Vernes' fictional novel,* Around the World in Eighty Days. *She was the only female reporter to attend Joseph Pulitzer's funeral.*

'Nellie Bly' is the title of a popular song composed by Stephen Foster (July 4, 1826-January 13, 1864) and published in 1850. Foster was born in Pittsburgh's Lawrenceville neighborhood and resided in Allegheny City and Pittsburgh. His body is buried in Pittsburgh's Allegheny Cemetery.

Fall 1886

Sarah's Early Column In The New York World

We have come a long way toward a new way of life, all of us, and it wasn't an accident. By that I mean our country has developed a sense of excitement and purpose since its founding a short one hundred and ten years ago, in 1776. I witnessed our growth. We all loved it, and it was inevitable: Our country's impressive industrial base, built largely during the thirty years or so after The Civil War, was and remains ready for more hyper-active development.

I witnessed it recently when I traveled by rail from New York City to Pittsburgh and its abutting suburb across the Allegheny River to the north, Allegheny City. I rode on the same rails that carried Pittsburgh industrialists to our city for conferences with bankers and lawyers. I was fortunate enough to travel in Henry Clay Frick's Pullman car, a true luxury in this day and age with its mahogany paneling, full kitchen and bar, sleeping berths, and waiters and butlers to satisfy our every need. Carnegie and Frick are close associates. Frick's firm, in fact, supplies Carnegie's steel mills with coke, a coal byproduct that is a critical ingredient in steel making.

I made the trip west for two reasons: to confirm that we live in a country that is so big and beautiful that it defies description (we do) and to see first-hand what I had heard: that the Pittsburgh/Allegheny City area is a frenetic cauldron of industrial and sports activity (it is). Upon my return, I wrote:

Thank you, boredom and confusion. You are the silent, unstoppable force behind the new and more exciting, pleasurable way of life. You are a creative mover and shaker of new lifestyles. If necessity is the mother of invention, boredom and confusion are the mother of sports and entertainment. Without you, we may still be drawing pictures on the walls of caves, kicking inflated pig's bladders through makeshift wickets, and hitting rocks with sticks.

Until the mid-1800s, residents of Allegheny City, Pittsburgh, and in fact all of Pennsylvania and America, spent their rare leisure time in assorted contests of skill without standardized rules. The universities and athletic clubs, euphemistically called social clubs, increasingly became sites for recreation such as games and the universal escape from harsh realities, drinking beer, whiskey, and other mind-bending beverages. These organizations tried to bring sense and order to random activities by applying standardized rules to the new games, particularly the evolving sports of baseball and football. The rules were adopted and refined, teams were formed, and the games were played.

Citizens attended sporting events and Church services—it

seems that every ethnic group has its own Church—for relief from incessant, pressing demands for finding the basics for a sparse existence—food, clothing, and shelter. Leisure time was a privilege for the wealthy few or a reward for arduous, dangerous work. Pastimes that measure speed such as track and horse racing; and reward, agility and eye-hand coordination such as tennis, archery, and soccer, all imported from Europe, became more popular. But they were unorganized and teams from different areas, even those nearby, played by their own, makeshift rules. It was impossible to hold contests with meaningful winners and losers.

Yet, winners, losers, and the thrills of competition were important, and still are. The self-worth of citizens, cities, even countries—in fact, their very identity, was and still is often shaped by their favorite athlete or team. We root and shout and fume at games at a primitive level, programmed to define and separate *us* from *them*, friends from foes, allies from enemies as we would in a war. We wear our hero's jerseys to make their identities our own. In short, we worship those we admire and wish we could be them, if only for a few fleeting minutes or hours.

A new sense of opportunity for wealth and happiness

We can thank President Abraham Lincoln for laying the groundwork for the phenomenal, unprecedented, flamboyant growth of America's economy, its enviable innovation, and its growing population. He noted, in the mid-1800s, that for the first time in human history it was possible for prudent, penniless beginners to become independent businessmen with discretionary money and time to spend it.

*

> *Abe was not being politically incorrect by referring to 'businessmen' instead of 'businesspersons' as we would say today. Most women in the 1800s were confined to being homemakers, mothers, clerks, or nurses. Nellie Bly and Sarah Scrivener opened new career opportunities for women by demonstrating that women can be as adventuresome and intelligent as men.*

*

Although not the norm, Abe's *prudent, penniless beginners* would labor for wages and save any surplus cash to buy tools or land, then work for their own wealth and happiness. Then, if successful, this epitome of entrepreneurship would hire another prudent, penniless beginner to help him bank even more greenbacks or gold, birthing a business and his financial and social independence. Such was, and remains, the course for many professional athletes.

Abe's prescient optimism—his vision for a greater, united America populated by entrepreneurs—was surely prompted and nurtured by the success of creative individuals and firms such as manufacturers of gun stocks for the military and grist mills for farmers and food processors. The result was a consensus among government and military officials that advanced technology must be (or should be) a national priority. It spurred the Industrial Revolution and the astonishing growth of basic Industries such as mining and smelting, steel-making and fabrication, oil exploration and production, automobiles and roads, and much more. . . the stuff of modern society.

It attracted immigrants from around the world, and it created employment with living wages. Eventually, workers had free time and discretionary cash.

*

More than a century-and -a half later, we call our national priority advanced technology, artificial Intelligence, medicine/healthcare, robotics, self-driving cars, and STEM--Science, Technology, Engineering, Math. Where are The Arts? I hope and predict that soon works of art, music, and literature will be welcomed into the broad realm of technology.

*

This sense of progress is founded on new priorities and opportunities; it permeated the amateur sports clubs and athletes, spurring entrepreneurship and larger enterprises than Abe or his associates could have imagined. *Entrepreneur, employer,* and *employee* became job descriptions in addition to being commercial endeavors and choices.

Such was life in Allegheny City, Pennsylvania, and throughout America. The country was still recovering from the traumas of The Civil War, aided immeasurably by innovative technologies and conveniences: Dirt streets rutted by carriage wheels turned into mud at the lightest rain were replaced by gravel, asphalt, and wood planks. Barges laden with oil pumped from wells owned by John D. Rockefeller, reputed to be the richest man in the world; coal, sand, iron ore and other minerals as well as furs and other luxury goods plied the waterways on large barges where only a lifetime ago birch bark canoes rode low in the water; and 3.5 million enslaved African American were freed when Lincoln signed the Emancipation, on January 1, 1863.

The vast, open lands around Allegheny City were mined for their coal. Blast furnaces and steel mills lined the rivers to be close to river transportation of their raw materials and for cooling their massive smelting equipment such as blast furnaces and open hearths. Railroads were becoming a way to transport goods and people, replacing the horse with the iron horse. It foretold the age of steam and steel and unimaginable wealth for tycoons such as steelmaker Andrew Carnegie, oil producer and refiner John D. Rockefeller, banker and venture capitalist J. P. Morgan, and railroad manipulator Jay Gould and his robber baron partners at The Erie Railroad.

Perhaps Allegheny City was the epicenter, the very heart, of this tectonic shift. Certainly to it was its image, its alter ego.

*

The Tycoons cooperated with each other to create wealth. One example: Railroads needed immense quantities of steel rails to construct many miles of new track that connected the country's far-flung coasts, cities, hamlets, towns, and farms. The rails were supplied by just over one thousand mills, many of them small and inefficient. As a result, large plants such as Carnegie's Edgar Thompson Works just upstream from Pittsburgh on the Monongahela River produced the bulk of it. Edgar Thompson was president of The Pennsylvania Railroad, a large purchaser of steel rails. Carnegie rewarded him, in a clear case of quid pro quo (cronyism?) with the name of his largest and most efficient plant, automatically making him a prominent part of the history of the railroad and steel industries. J. P. Morgan participated with massive amounts of capital and Gould with massive amounts of chicanery. By the way, The ET Works is still operating a century later as an important part of United States Steel, the first company with annual revenue of more than a billion dollars. (1901, $1.4 billion, about $4 per person in America)

But Perhaps this dynasty is ending. At the time of this writing, Nippon Steel of Japan has offered to buy U.S. Steel. Is Carnegie turning in his grave?

View Of Pittsburgh And Allegheny Pennsylvania, 1874

2.
BIRTHING MODERN FOOTBALL AND THE VISIONARIES WHO MADE IT HAPPEN

Men and boys risked injury, pain, and death for love of a violent game. Hints of professionalism were ignored by The Amateur Athletic Union (AAU). Owners circumvented the rules with hidden and disguised payments to players.

Allegheny City, Pennsylvania   January 20, 1890

The Pittsburgh Chronicle and Telegraph

Meet Sarah Scrivener, Our New Senior Reporter

By Joseph Siebeneck, editor

I am pleased to announce that Sarah Scrivener has joined the paper as Senior Reporter. Sarah was formerly Cub Reporter at *The New York World*, where she worked with Joseph Pulitzer to enhance his reputation as champion for the common person and to sell more papers than William Randolph Hearst and his *New York Journal*. She also honed her distinctive hard-hitting prose style that appeals so much to a wide range of readers. I know that she will continue that same stance while with us here in our growing and vibrant city.

Sarah will cover and record the notable events here, including the stirrings of new politics led by our ambitious Mayor, the Honorable Richard Turner Pearson. She will also investigate and report on our vibrant businesses and entertainments such as our emerging sports scene at Recreation Park nearby, built in 1876, and the newer and larger Exposition Park on the edge of the Allegheny River.

She is professionally qualified to do so. She grew up with seven brothers who insisted that she join them and their neighbors playing stick ball—cricket's cousin and the forerunner of our baseball. She is also quite apt at soccer, the forerunner of our football that is so popular in many European countries. To be modest, she is quite well known and respected on the streets of New York City for her athleticism, as I am certain she will be here.

Her sports credentials continue. She was stellar at field hockey and track while attending Syracuse University's School of Journalism, from which she graduated with honors. The Governor of New York and the faculty are still talking about her stirring commencement speech. Frankly, it is one reason I asked her to join the paper.

She covered sports for *The World*, and, not surprisingly, became dedicated to physical fitness. You will recognize her for her thin face with delicate, smooth features and her slim, agile, athletic form that rivals those of our best athletes.

You might recognize her as well for her tasteful, colorful silk taffeta dress, flat in front and bustled in back in conformance with recent styles. She looks like she just stepped out of the pages of the chicest fashion magazine from New York or Paris. You will know her by her extraordinarily long dark hair and penetrating eyes that shine with curiosity and intelligence.

You will recognize Sarah as well on our streets or in our many restaurants. She'll be carrying a notepad and pencil in her left hand, ready to chronicle interesting events as she finds them.

Please say hello and welcome her to our city.

When you engage her in conversation, you will recognize her for her gruff, casual, saucy language of sports, one of her many endearing qualities that she displays while always maintaining her ladylike demeanor and professionalism under all circumstances.

She is the personification of 'Tom Boy'.

Readers can expect controversial stories that stir imagination and thinking, stories that appeal through short, provocative headlines and sentences written in a breezy and friendly style.

Although controversial, you can expect her columns to be open and honest, adhering to the highest levels of journalistic integrity. I expect her to call for reforms in our government and sports—she strongly advocates sportsmanlike, ethical behavior by our politicians in and out of their posh offices and athletes on and off the field. In short, she will report on the activities in all parts of our evolving society when and wherever needed.

Please look for her columns in future editions of this paper and let me know how you like them. I feel quite certain that you will be entertained and enlightened. Nevertheless, she and I welcome your recommendations for improvement.

*

Sports buffs and serious historians have debated for years who played the first college football game. Many believe that it took place when Harvard and Tufts tussled on June 4, 1875 on Jarvis Field in Cambridge, Massachusetts. Others believe football as we know it now was developed at Harvard as long ago as 1863. This game, known as The Boston Game, *included catching and running with the ball, keys to the development of the non-soccer type game in America.* Tufts won that game against Harvard, 1-0. At the time, a touchdown was awarded one point.

Still other sports buffs declare that Rutgers and Princeton played the first intercollegiate football game between two American colleges on November 6, 1869, but that game was played with rules akin to contemporary soccer. Players couldn't run with the ball or tackle opponents, so it is a stretch to call it football.

Syracuse University, Sarah's alma mater, was slow to join the furor over football: Its football team played its first game on November 23,1889 against The Medical College of Syracuse. The team was called The Orange Orioles, then Hillmen Bills, Orange Men, and finally, The Orange with blue as a secondary color. The colors were proposed after Syracuse trounced Hamilton College. Players and students wanted colors as bold as they were. The name stuck.

Regardless, football's increasing popularity among players and fans is exemplified by The Rose Bowl. It was first played in 1902 in Pasadena, California, as the Tournament East-West Football Game. and has been played every year since 1916. Attendance has consistently been higher than at any other football game. Alabama won the first game, defeating Michigan 27-20 in overtime.

*

Allegheny City, Pennsylvania   February 15, 1890

My Gratitude Is Boundless.

By Sarah Scrivener, Senior Reporter

Thank you, citizens of Allegheny City. A confession: I am in love with Allegheny City and all of you whom I have met and will soon. Since I joined *The Pittsburgh Chronicle and Telegraph* only three weeks ago, you have made me feel comfortable in my new home and career. You have removed any fear I might have had moving hundreds of miles from the turmoil of crowded New York City to the relative calm of Allegheny City and Western Pennsylvania.

I love your friendliness and ambitions. Your city, and now mine, has grown from humble beginnings as a colonial outpost and agricultural center to be, alongside Pittsburgh, one of the most important cities in the World and a driver behind America's bustling economy. I suspect that you will be a driver of organized sports such as football and baseball, and of other forms of entertainment.

I feel compelled to begin my tenure here with a brief history of football, which, along with baseball, I am betting will become an important if not dominant sport and source of entertainment within the next decade. I say that since football is so grand in scope. If I may be poetic for a minute, it is the melding of sport and society. It is our soul, a reflection of our very psyche. Regrettably, it satisfies our need to win at any cost for many of us.

The current game combines rugby and soccer and is played mostly by robust college students in their late teens and early twenties, less by members of the many athletic clubs that are springing up all over America, particularly in New York, Chicago, Cleveland, and Saint Louis. And now, here. We have joined the fray and most of us are happy that we have.

However, all is not rosy; there are ugly, dangerous downsides lurking within the game itself and with the people who are managing it.

For those of you who are not familiar with the sport, its purpose is to acquire territory using force, much like the purpose of war. It's rough and tumble style appeals to the darker, dangerous side of our nature. You could say and hope that it replaces war, which is of course desirable and certainly within our reach.

Football by its very nature is violent. Teams move the ball up the field by ramming full speed into the opposing team, a crude tactic that causes many injuries and a few deaths every season.

Players, despite being well-padded, typically by bulky 'uniforms' sewn at home by tolerant wives and mothers, risk losing life, limbs, and teeth, and breaking bones every time they take the field. They play for the love of the game, as well as to satisfy their need for conquest, to be the best, to win, and have fun.

Which brings me to Walter Camp, the former star player at Yale and now an extraordinarily successful coach. He deserves his own column for his profound influence on the game and on many of our local players. I'll talk to him about it.

Walter Chauncey Camp

In addition, he has interjected more finesse into the game to replace brute force. He has written extensive rules and invented such tactics as the forward pass to replace and supplement constant ramming and running. He has added some sense of civility that may accelerate the game and reduce the number and severity of injuries.

I see him as the father of the game and will write more about him in future columns. Please look for them. I expect the game to catch on here and throughout America.

*

At least two football traditions were born in 1890: In March, Ohio State University played its first football game, in Delaware, Ohio, beating Ohio Wesleyan 20-14. In November the US Navy trounced Army, 24-0 at West Point, in the first Army-Navy game.

Also in 1890, Journalist Nellie Bly completed her journey around the world in 72 days (about 2 and a half months), several days ahead of schedule, and Chicago was chosen by a committee to be the site for the Columbian Exposition .It will open in Spring 1893 and feature a massive Ferris Wheel that was conceived at a luncheon in Chicago and designed in Allegheny City and Pittsburgh by George Ferris and his brilliant junior engineer, William Gronau. He joined George's engineering firm in the Summer of 1887, just after graduating from Rensselaer Polytech Institute (RPI) as a civil engineer. His initial assignments were to inspect bridge materials in Massillon and Mount Vernon Ohio, Pittsburgh, Chicago, Cleveland, and other locations.

In April 1889, George broadened William's responsibilities and promoted him to engineer in charge of bridge design, and subsequently

George named Gruoau and David McNaugher, another RPI graduate, partners in G. W. G Ferris Engineering Company.

*

While designing the Wheel, Gronau developed new methods for calculating and proving stresses for large tension wheels, a first in engineering that contributed to the design of skyscrapers. He later co-founded, with John Gray, another RPI graduate but with a degree in architecture, Gray and Gronau, architects and bridge engineers. Gronau is only one of many engineers who went on to successful careers that George trained and encouraged.

*

First Army-Navy Football Game

36 | Birthing Modern Football

Allegheny City, Pennsylvania   May 15, 1890

The Allegheny Athletic Association (AAA) emerges with promises of greatness.

By Sarah Scrivener, Senior Reporter

Joseph Siebeneck, my boss as editor/owner of *The Pittsburgh Chronicle and Telegraph*, and I were chatting in the parlor of the Siebeneck home on the corner of Beech and Galveston Avenues in Allegheny City. It was early in May 1890, and I had arrived a few short months before from New York City, where I was employed as a reporter by Joseph Pulitzer and his *New York World* after graduating from the Syracuse University School of Journalism. I love writing and sports., and I love being able to communicate with my readers.

"You will not be bored here, I assure you," said Siebeneck. "The area is growing rapidly and our Mayor, James Wyman, is only a month into his second term. He is ambitious. He plans to encourage new industry—you've heard of George Westinghouse and his marvelous air brake which is made only a few blocks away—I hear that he and his scientists are developing an electric light bulb to rival Edison's, and that George is negotiating a contract to supply thousands of them to the upcoming Columbian EXPO in Chicago. I also hear that home builders are planning to install electricity in existing and new larger and more luxurious homes, starting in Braddock, one of Pittsburgh's more affluent Eastern suburbs.

"We're proud of our universities, and our budding industrial base and sports scene. Several of our residents recently formed The Allegheny Athletic Association. They have ambitious plans for football and baseball games at our Exposition and Recreation Parks down by The Allegheny River."

A few weeks after my conversation with Mister Siebeneck I met with four of the players on the Allegheny Athletic Association (AAA) football team and am impressed with their enthusiasm and skills. Many of them had attended prestigious eastern colleges and played football. Two, Oliver David Thompson (OD) and John Moorhead, played at Yale with Walter Camp, who I predict will go down in history as an imaginative inventor of the rules of the game as well as an outstanding player. And to think he has done all that at only 156 pounds. I heard that an uncouth Harvard player took one look at Camp and asked Yale's captain, Gene Baker, "you don't mean to let that child play, do you? He will get hurt." Not only did Camp play, but he also played halfback with such fervor and distinction that he was named coach of the team in 1888, when his team won the national championship.

AAA's quarterback is Abram Sharpless Valentine, who prefers to be called AS. He played at The University of Pennsylvania and deserves special attention as the dirtiest player in college football. I predict that he will continue to play with unsportsmanlike vigor while with AAA, which is surely unethical but within the current rules of the game. I hope that he will mend his ways in the future, but I doubt it. I do not doubt that he will help win many games for AAA and put our city on the map, I hope favorably.

AAA's backfield boasts Harry Oliver and Harry Fry at halfback and OD Thompson at fullback and manager, the first player/manager that I know of. Like many of his peers, OD attended Yale where he played halfback, fullback, and tackle alongside Walter Camp. OD and Walter can be thought of as the co-inventors of the forward pass, a story that I will pass on to you in the near future.

I am sorry to report that despite its illustrious backfield, AAA cannot give its cross-town rivals, the East End Gymnasium Club, a proper battle. So, OD stepped up recruiting and arranged for a game against Western University of Pittsburgh, a team staffed with younger and inexperienced players who are supposedly easier to beat.

AAA isn't the only athletic club in America or even Western Pennsylvania. At about the same time it was created, athletic clubs and football teams were being organized in towns surrounding Pittsburgh such as Greensburg, Erie, and Latrobe, and in larger cities such as New York, Saint Louis, and Chicago.

*

Oliver David Thompson, aka OD Thompson, played halfback, fullback, and tackle at Yale from 1876-1878, a few years before Pudge Heffelfinger began his storied career there. Walter Camp is credited with developing—inventing football based on his knowledge and love of rugby. After Yale, OD returned to the Pittsburgh area (he was born in Butler, Pennsylvania, only about fifteen miles north) and played for AAA before becoming player/manager from 1890-1892, and 1893-1896. He recorded his historic signing of Pudge in a ledger that was uncovered in the 1960s with this line: "Game performance bonus to W. Heffelfinger for playing (cash) $500."

OD and Walter are known also for executing the first forward pass in a game pitting Yale against Princeton played in Hoboken, New Jersey. Camp ran for a good gain and, as he was being tackled, threw the ball forward to OD who ran for a touchdown. Princeton protested that the play was illegal, i.e. it violated the rules. But there were no rules for forward passes or, if there were, they were unclear, and the play was allowed only when Yale won a referee's coin toss. Thus, a big part of modern football's offense is based on an anonymous flip of a coin many years ago.

*

Oliver David Thompson 1906

October 11, 1890

In what may be the first official football game in Allegheny City and Pittsburgh, AAA and The Western University of Pittsburgh (renamed the University of Pittsburgh in 1908) clashed at Exposition Park. OD's recruiting paid off. AAA won the game easily, 38-0 in front of 500 rabid fans including the mayor of Allegheny City, the Honorable James Wyman. He took office in April with promises of eliminating corruption and supporting local sports teams. I hope that he succeeds.

All eleven of the starting AAA players like to be thought of as residents of Allegheny City or Pittsburgh. They aren't. The team is a motley, diverse collection of local and nearby athletes posing as a team. Some traveled here from as far away as Greensburg, Latrobe, and Jeanette, where they also play for the local athletic clubs. Love of the game is everywhere in our area.

October 18, 1890

AAA defeated Shady Side Academy today, 32-0, proving that its rout of The Western University of Pittsburgh team a week ago was not a fluke as some worthy, misguided pundits have hinted. In fact, I feel quite certain that AAA will go on to be one of the premier football teams in Pennsylvania if not the eastern states and as far west as Cleveland.

AAA controlled the game against Shady Side for the entire sixty minutes of play. Our linemen dominated theirs. In fact, I could say that our guys pushed theirs out of the way so our stellar running backs could run amok. It was fun to watch. I expect more of the same: AAA is loaded with talent, OD Thompson at full back in particular.

By the way, and in the interests of my reporting baseball as well as football events, if you didn't know, on September 30, only two weeks ago, The Brooklyn Bridegrooms clinched the National League pennant. I'll report on their performance in subsequent columns, but for now suffice to say that their worthy opponent is AAA's nemesis, The Louisville Colonels.

December 1, 1890

OOPS! I may have been a bit hasty when I predicted that AAA would be one of the premier football teams in a wide area centered in Allegheny City. Only four weeks ago, on November first, an inexperienced Princeton Preparatory team embarrassed AAA by 44-6, the worst loss in the team's brief history. Then AAA tied the Detroit Athletic Club and lost, 6-4, to the Cleveland Athletic Club, both amateur squads AAA should have beaten easily. Nevertheless, I stick to my prediction and confidence in the AAA players and managers and declare, along with my editor, AAA to be the local champion this season.

Allegheny Athletic Association football team, 1892. Back row: Sutton, Harry H. Rowand, William J. Kountz Jr. Middle row: Norman McClintock, Henry Floy, William W. Blunt, Frank R. Coates, Abram S. Valentine, Delevan Emery. Front row: Fred W. Albree, John Boden, Thomas Ewing Jr., Charles Donnelly Jr.

*

In 1890 a touchdown was awarded five points, a goal from touchdown (extra point) one point, a goal from the field (field goal) four points, and a safety two points. A forward pass was rare, considered to be trickery bordering on being illegal., and the games incredibly dangerous.

Players risked severe injury on just about every play. (In 1905, for example, nineteen players died from football injuries) and Teddy Roosevelt would have banned the sport if a committee of sports lovers from more than sixty universities had not met to discuss safety. The committee, chaired by Walter Camp, voted to ban the flying wedge, reduce playing time from 70 to 60 minutes, and create the National Collegiate Athletic Association (NCAA) to oversee compliance with safety and other rules of play.

*

The 1905 Big Game at Stanford Field

During the season, I was privileged to know many of the players, among them John Moorhead. John played for Yale during the late 1870s, and later for AAA in 1890 when he played center beside OD who played tackle. OD was an early member of the club and, later, its coach and president. Both Moorhead and OD played at Yale alongside Walter Camp, who deserves the special mention I gave him in another column.

Walter, as I write this, is the young and phenomenally successful coach at Yale. I predict that he will influence football in many ways before he retires.

By the way again, we were not the only football pioneers. At the risk of repeating my comments in an earlier column, on June 4, 1869, eleven years ago, Harvard and Tufts (The university founded by circus showman P.T. Barnum) clashed in one of the first games that would be recognizable as played under modern rules, other sources posit that the first American football game was played on November 6, 1869, between Rutgers and New jersey, soon to become Princeton. Rutgers won, 6-4.

On March 3 of this year (1890) the first American football game in Ohio State University history was played in Delaware, Ohio, against Ohio Wesleyan University. It was a close game. Ohio State won by 20-14. Eight months later, on November 29, the Army and Navy clashed for the first time. Navy trounced Army 24-0, on 'The Plain' at West Point.

I predict many such contests in coming years, and Army versus Navy will become one of the enduring traditional rivalries in college football.

January 21, 1891

A new year, a new set of opportunities to report the many events here in Allegheny City and

Pittsburgh. I again visited Joseph Siebeneck, my editor, to discuss the burgeoning football and baseball scene. It seems that in the East End of Pittsburgh—reputed to be the richest neighborhood in the world with an extraordinarily high percentage of millionaires that is only six or so miles east of Allegheny City—a group of athletes called the East Enders formed the Pittsburgh Athletic Club (PAC) to play football and compete with AAA.

As you can imagine, finances and jealousy played their ugly roles. The athletes at PAC understood that AAA was coining money by selling tickets to their exciting games played at Exposition Park and figured that they could too with games at East Liberty Park. AAA's football team also added to the prestige of the club and membership soared to more than 330 persons, the same as East End's, igniting a bitter rivalry for paying members and fans as well as winning football games.

Many of us are aware that athletic clubs such as the AAA and East End Gymnasium Club in Pittsburgh have become social centers in neighborhoods all over America. AAA is built around OD Thompson, a marvelous and versatile athlete who plays center and manages the team. The East End Gymnasium Club is built around its physical director—some note that his title is Instructor of Gymnastics and Physical Culture—Luis Frederick Kirchner, an offensive lineman reputed to be the best in Pennsylvania. I will tell readers more

Kirchner from 1904 Washington & Jefferson College yearbook

about this marvelous athlete and physical specimen in a subsequent column. I am certain that we will hear more from both OD and Louis in the future, just as I am certain that sports will become more popular and our national pastime, perhaps our obsession for pleasure and relaxation.

November 1891

The East Enders closed their first season undefeated at 7-0. Harry Fry, who toils in AAA's and East End's backfield, starred in the opener and then throughout the season. He is a marvelous athlete. The managers of the team showed their appreciation for the outstanding record and presented each player with a gold watch in the shape of a football that also serves as a trophy. I am sure that the players will cherish them.

October 1892, Columbus Day,

On this 400th anniversary of Columbus' discovery of America, PAC and AAA faced each other for the first time. It was a titanic struggle that ended in a 6-6 tie. The game was riddled with accusations of professionalism and of subterfuge. Adding drama to an already dramatic event, PAC accused AAA players of intentionally trying to injure PAC's star center, Luis Kirchner, and they might have succeeded when Kirchner left the game with a dysfunctional ankle. AAA, not to be outdone, accused PAC, especially Kirchner, to be a paid professional and should not have been in the lineup.

Meanwhile, PAC's captain, Charley Aull, who played guard and quarterback from 1889 until 1891 for Penn State, had quietly signed a sub center, a man named Stayer. It turned out that 'Stayer' is really A. C. Read, the captain of the Penn State team. Although nobody can prove that Read was paid and PAC had not tried to pass him as a member of the club, it added fire to an already incendiary situation, and neither club would hesitate to violate the AAU rules and hire players for hard cash and other incentives.

Despite the rancor, the teams scheduled a rematch to be played at Recreation Park in Allegheny City. Anything for sport, fun, and money, eh?

November 12, 1892

PAC faced AAA for the second time this season. AAA won, 4-0, when Pudge Heffelfinger, an outstanding guard and athlete and 3-time All American at Yale, picked up a fumble and ran into the end zone. I was at that game along with about 500 other rabid residents of the area and I must tell you it was the hardest fought and exciting that I have ever witnessed. Perhaps the bloodiest too. Many players sported bloody noses and missing teeth—their helmets did not protect their faces and I daresay that they did little to protect their heads. Body padding was equally ineffective. A few players limped off the field, some holding their dangling arms.

When Pudge picked up that fumble and scored, the stadium erupted with a roar that I can only describe as deafening. Honestly, I thought that Recreation Park would shake to pieces. Football, I think, could very well become our national pastime, certainly our national passion just as soccer is in several European countries.

OD invited me to his home for a cup of tea and glass of beer after the game where I met a handsome fellow named George Ferris and his gorgeous wife Margaret, a dark-haired beauty. They live on Arch Street, very near my editor's home. I learned that George owns and manages an engineering company headquartered on Grant Street in Pittsburgh and is working on a contract to test the materials that are used to build the huge Columbian Exposition in Chicago.

He is finalizing a contract to design and build a huge rotating vertical wheel that will carry more than two thousand people to unprecedented heights and views of Chicago itself. He told me that he got the idea for the wheel while attending a luncheon in Chicago during which the project manager, an architect named Daniel Burnham, challenged the engineers to imagine and then design and build a national icon that would rival, even outshine, the Eiffel Tower in Paris. Quite a challenge, I would say. I cannot wait to see what he comes up with.

Our discussion that evening also touched on the growth and wealth of Allegheny City. Our population had grown to 105,000 residents (about the seating capacity of the Los Angeles Memorial Coliseum), up from a mere 28, 702 in 1860, including, according to *The New York Tribune's American Millionaires,* an astounding 44 millionaires living right under our noses. No question that since 1860 our economy boomed with no end in sight. Congratulations to all of you who made it happen, with special thanks to Elizabeth and Harry Thaw (a railroad baron, chairman of the Hecla Coal Company, and one of our 44 millionaires) who graciously rented me a small apartment in their mansion on North Lincoln Avenue. Amazingly comfortable.

*

Harry Thaw achieved eternal infamy as the jealous lover of Evelyn Nesbit, a teenage cabaret performer. Thaw shot and killed Sanford White, architect and Evelyn's lover, in front of a crowd. The episode became the movie, The Girl in the Red Velvet Swing. The Thaw Mansion became offices, apartments, and an art studio.

Allegheny City, Pennsylvania   December 15, 1895

The First Professional Football Player? Let the debate begin.

Many contenders duke it out for their place in history.

By Sarah Scrivener

Ever since men first challenged each other in an arena, on the playing field, or in the jungle to determine who could bring home the biggest mammoth or trout, they have debated who is or was the best at their skill. Surely the Greeks debated who was the best marathoner and gladiator, the Brits the best cricketeer and polo player, the Canadians the best curlers, the early Americans the best hunters, fishers, and farmers, and so on. Today, in our enlightened mid-1890s, our debates often focus on who was the first professional, i.e. paid, football player, and is or was he the most skilled at his position. We don't have a quick or easy answer. Too many of them are or were good to best at their positions.

I've been covering sports here in Allegheny City and at times the surrounding area for the past several years and have been honored to meet any number of fine athletes and entered may debates about which are the best. By the way, the best place for a hot debate of this nature is the nearby Drover's Hotel, reputed to be where George Ferris dropped in occasionally for a refreshing beer and decided to marry Margaret as he sipped a brew with his friend and partner, another RPI graduate engineer. Great bar with powers of persuasion.

At the same time, 1895, Nikolai Tesla and George Westinghouse designed and built the first hydro-electric power station in Niagara Falls. It accelerated the electrification of America and made manufacturing more productive and efficient. Countless new products became economically feasible to make, helping to spur The Age of the Consumer. At the Niagara plant's opening ceremony on January 12, 1897, Tesla said:

"We have many a monument of past ages; we have the palaces and pyramids, the temples of the Greek and the cathedrals of Christendom. In them is exemplified the power of men, the greatness of nations, the love of art and religious devotion. But the monument at Niagara has something of its own, more in accord with our present thoughts and tendencies. It is a monument worthy of our scientific age, a true monument of enlightenment and of peace. It signifies the subjugation of natural forces to the service of man, the discontinuance of barbarous methods, the relieving of millions from want and suffering."

*

Readers can only imagine how animated and fun the debates over "the best athletes" are. One such debate that absolutely has the life of Methuselah and the fury of a gladiator has been which player was the first to be paid, i.e. to break from the ranks of amateurs and become professional. Two conclusions are that we may never know who was first, and the best players are also the most likely to be paid, or to be paid more than their teammates.

*

Players were paid extraordinarily little during this era. One star, despite his fame both locally and nationally, lived in a boarding house in a neighborhood of aging homes, smoking manufacturing plants, and noisy trains racing down railroad tracks embedded in muddy streets. Many of his teammates rented rooms in the same or nearby neighborhood, and others boarded in a fleabag hotel. The star pitcher and lifelong Pittsburgher, Frank Killen, lived alone in an unpretentious brick home in the Mexican War Streets and rode streetcars to Recreation and Exposition Parks.

Players needed a second job to live decently. Some were bartenders in the many pubs, others menial workers in plants such as George Westinghouse's air brake plant. Still others were salesclerks in local shops or teachers/physical fitness coaches in nearby schools. Very few, if any, lived comfortably or in conditions approaching luxury.

*

At least six football players have credible claims of being the first to be paid, the first to break from the ranks of amateurs from 1889 to today, a span of six years that spawned many changes to the game and many outstanding players.

My six contenders:

Louis Frederick Kirchner

(July 1865 - June 1951) is an obvious choice to be the first pro football player, the first pro athlete in any sport. He surely is one of the greatest, most deserving. He is a true Renaissance Man and an asset to his hometown, Pittsburgh and the several teams for which he played.

In 1889 Louis joined the East End Gymnastics Club as a coach in charge of gymnastics and physical culture. In 1890, he was one of the first to join the new football team, the Pittsburgh Athletic Club, a spin-off of the East End Gymnastics Club. It was headquartered in the East End of a growing Pittsburgh, now its Oakland and East Liberty neighborhoods. He played center and guard and was acclaimed by peers, fans, and especially opponents, as one of the best linemen in Pennsylvania, if not the best, including Pudge Heffelfinger who was at the time a standout guard playing at Yale University.

In 1890 Louis played, along with Grant Dibert, at center for pickup teams called The East Enders and the All Pittsburghs, and seven games for Allegheny Athletic Association (AAA) in Allegheny City. AAA's manager,

OD Thompson, convinced him to play guard, ostensibly to recreate Pudge's astronomical success at that position at Yale.

Between 1890 and 1892 the local media hinted—they had to have known, it was so obvious—that Kirchner and certain of his team-mates were paid to play. The hints were certainly not the first media cover-up, this one to preserve the amateur status of AAA and PAC. Regardless, the sports writers of the day—were they in on the scam?—hinted that Kirchner and others on the two Pittsburgh teams were masquerading as amateurs when in truth they were being paid as professionals. For proof, they noted that Kirchner's salary as a professor at a local university rose—some sources say it doubled—as the number of classes he taught declined, doubling his income and opening his schedule to play football. It was a covert double whammy that succeeded in preserving his and his team's amateur status.

The Amateur Athletic Union, which existed to examine such anomalies in its attempts to preserve amateurism, instead ignored them for unknown reasons.

If the AAU had investigated, Kirchner likely would have found greater fame (there is nothing like a scandal for generating publicity) and been named to the football hall of fame as the first professional football player instead of, or as well as, Pudge Heffelfinger.

When his playing days ended. Kirchner, who had earned an MD from the Western University of Pittsburgh and resigned from his job as PAC's athletic instructor to accept a similar position at Washington and Jefferson College a few miles south of Pittsburgh. His responsibilities soon expanded to include coach of the basketball and track teams and professor of hygiene. He retired from W & J in 1941 and died in 1951 in his mid eighties.

Ira Lawson Fiscus

(1866 - 1949) and his brother Ross played well enough at Indiana Normal School (soon to be Indiana University of Pennsylvania) to be paid 'liberal expense money' by AAA. In 1892 Ira played guard and halfback at Princeton so aggressively and fiercely that his teammates and the media dubbed him *The Samson of Princeton*. He left Princeton at the end of the 1892 season and returned to his home in Indiana Pennsylvania and play, in 1893, for AAA and the Greensburg Athletic Association, which secretly offered him $20 per game, anointing it the third football team in three years to hire professionals after AAA and PAC. Lawson is the sixth player known to have been paid openly to play football.

Lawson dabbled unsuccessfully in various businesses when his playing days ended. He eventually became police chief of Youngwood Pennsylvania, an exurb southeast of Pittsburgh.

William "Pudge" Heffelfinger

(December 20, 1867 - April 2 1954) could be the greatest, most punishing guard ever to play the game, sharing those accolades with Kirchner. Standing six feet, three inches tall and weighing a hefty 200 pounds of solid muscle, Pudge is definitely not pudgy. He towers over his teammates and rival players, wreaks havoc on opposing players, and can take out two or three of them at a time during one play from scrimmage. He has proved to be a game changer many times.

Pudge played for Yale University—a major football power along with Harvard, Princeton, Penn, and Columbia—the future Ivy League. He toiled on both the offensive and defensive lines and was named to Walter Camp's All-American team three times. He led Yale to undefeated seasons in 1888 (when Yale outscored its opponents an incredible 698 to 0) and 1891, and to one-loss seasons in 1889 and 1890.

In November 1892, OD Thompson, manager of AAA, paid Pudge $500—about the same as a factory worker is paid for 3 months labor—to play one game against its bitter rival PAC. AAA won, 4-0, when Pudge picked up a fumble and ran 35 yards into the end zone for the game's only score.

When he quit playing, Pudge switched to coaching with stops at University of California, Lehigh University, and University of Minnesota. He also returned to Yale to help coach the current team on how to defeat Harvard. To diversify, he founded Heffelfinger publications which produced booklets to sell athletic equipment and worked in his father's shoe-making business. He was Minnesota's delegate to the Republican National Convention in 1904 and 1908 and ran unsuccessfully for US Congress in 1930.

*

Fast forward to 2023, when no self-respecting pro football player would toil for $500 a game or even its current inflation-adjusted stipend of about $14,000. Even the rawest rookie makes more. In fact, the minimum contemporary annual salary for a first-year professional football player is $750,000, or about $40,000 per game. Second year minimum salaries soar to $870,000 and third year to $940, 000.

*

Ben 'Sport' Donnelly

(October 18, 1869 - August 3, 1922) starred at end for Princeton and then played for a number of amateur and pro teams, including AAA during the 1892, 1893, and 1894 seasons. AAA paid him $250 to play one game, on November 19, 1892, against Washington and Jefferson College, only 7 days after AAA paid Pudge $500 for the same task. A year later AAA hired Ben to be player/coach, making him the first to coach a known pro team. He then served for one season, 1893, as the second head football coach at the University of Iowa.

"Sport" was infamous for its unsportsmanlike, aka 'dirty' play. One of his favorite stunts was to purposely punch an opposing player and then tell the referee, "Watch this guy. He's been slugging me all day." When the opposing player retaliated it was under the keen eye of the ref, typically on the next play, and he was ejected from the game. Pudge, who was playing for Chicago at the time, said that Sport was the "only man he played against who could slug you and keep his eyes on the ball at the same time."

Ben is often credited with being the first pro football coach and second pro football player.

His playing days over, Ben became assistant coach at Purdue University in Lafayette Indiana under his friend and head coach Knowlton Ames. In 1891, the team coached by Ames and Donnelly won four games without a loss and outscored opponents 192-0. In 1892, their team won eight games without a loss and outscored opponents 320-24.

One year after AAA paid Pudge and Sport to play one game, PAC signed **Grant Dibert**, fullback (1869? - ?) to the first known pro contract. It stipulated that PAC pay Grant $50 per game for all the games PAC plays during the 1893 season. Grant agreed by writing, "I agree to participate in all regularly scheduled football games of The Pittsburg Athletic Club for the full season of 1893 ... As an active player I agree to accept a salary of $50 per contest and also acknowledge that I will play for no other club during PAC games." Unfortunately for Dibert, his star status didn't last long, and he was soon lost to history.

The Pittsburgh club denied that it paid anybody to play football, and the players apparently didn't admit to taking the money either.

As the *Pittsburg Herald* wrote, praising the manager and the president of the Allegheny team for maintaining the purity of amateur athletics: "[They] have done much toward making amateur sports and pastimes what they are in Pittsburg. ... They have always aimed at sports that are pure and ennobling. (implying that being paid makes sports impure and debasing) If all sports and contests were carried on according to their principles, there would be absolutely nothing dishonest or dishonoring in the sporting world today. They were athletes for the love of it, and they patronize athletics now because of the resultant benefits to athletes."

In one small way, Dibert played sports what they are today. We can thank him for that.

In one of the early apparent breaches of contract—it boggles the mind to think of how many have been breached since—Grant played one game for PAC and at least one game for AAA during the 1893 season, but nobody knows if he was paid by either club. What is known is that his punting was credited with pinning Cleveland back into its own half of the field, enabling AAA to win the game. He was an accomplished player as well as an accomplished bender of contractual obligations.

Dibert was a fullback at Swarthmore College in the late 1880s and played for the "All-Pittsburghs", an informal collection of local players, in a pick-up game against AAA. The following season, he remained with PAC but also played at least one game with AAA. He opened PACs 1893 season as a fullback but soon lost his position after the fourth game and was replaced, for unknown reasons, by an unknown sub. He did not play again for PAC. Nobody knows if he was paid for only the games he played or if he was paid a bribe to not play for AAA.

John Kinport "Sal" Brallier

(December 12, 1876-September 17, 1960) is nationally known as the first pro football player. In 1895, The Latrobe Pennsylvania Athletic Association (LAA) 'openly paid'—i.e. managers freely acknowledged that he was a professional. In contrast, OD hid payments to Pudge in an obscure ledger as he attempted to protect the amateur status of the team. If it had been taken away, all previous wins might have been erased from the record books.

In the Fall of 1895, when Sal was only 18 years old, LAA paid him $10 plus expenses to play against the Jeanette Athletic Association and promised to pay him for several other games and to throw in 'some cakes' to make it worthwhile. The teams were close neighbors, located in adjacent towns only a few miles east of Pittsburgh, but bitter rivals.

Sal arrived in Latrobe the night before the game and practiced with the team under a gas streetlight. The next day, Sal kicked two field goals to help LAA win the game, 12-0.

Sal played quarterback in high school, later at several universities, and then coached LAA from 1896-1902 to four undefeated seasons. His teams won 36 games, tied 4, and lost only three.

After football, John retired to Latrobe, where he was a dentist and school director for twenty years. After retiring in 1931, he traveled in parts of Florida and Canada. He was the last survivor of the Latrobe football team when he died in 1960.

Is My Choice Yours?

All the players named above are candidates to be the first pro, setting off an endless but hot, futile debate. I'll do my best to settle it for the last time. No question, it was Louis Frederick Kirchner, the greatest lineman in Pennsylvania, and perhaps, the country and the bulwark of the teams for which he played. He was the best ever, and was obviously being subsidized by someone, likely OD from the coffers of AAA. Pudge comes in a close second.

Poor Grant Dibert. He would be #1 if he had stuck to the terms of his contract, or would he? It's pure speculation. Sal Brallier comes in as #6, and the others somehow fall in between. If any readers want to debate this pressing issue, I will be at the bar in the Drovers Hotel every evening this week from 5 to 7. I look forward to meeting you and our discussions.

BUT ... my loyalties are to Allegheny City, and I admit to the bias. So, I would vote for Pudge only because he was paid here and won a game for our team. Anybody want to debate my choice?

Pudge Heffelfinger has emerged as the apparent winner in this charade only because two players/managers needed to hide payments to protect the amateur status of two players and teams. Surely their covert actions were at best unsportsmanlike for the times, and at worst unethical and a violation of contemporary rules set forth by the Amateur Athletic Union that would be punishable by reversing wins to losses. In at least one case, the AAU ignored the situation. Nobody knows why, which is another reason for debate. Could it be kick-backs?

Frankly, Pudge is widely acknowledged as the first pro because of an accident of timing and unintended secrecy, not a conspiracy by any means. Nevertheless, he is a talented player who deserves wide praise.

Honorable mention:

Walter Camp

(April 7, 1859 - March 14, 1925) the most versatile and influential player could be a candidate for *First Pro* by way of osmosis: He touched the lives of many players and managers, including many who have and are toiling for AAA and PAC, at times both simultaneously. Walter starred as a halfback at Yale between 1876 and 1881, five years during which he honed his techniques and ideas for rules and management. He starred as head coach of Yale in 1888, 1891, and 1892. During his tenure at Yale his teams won an amazing 67 games and lost only two.

He also coached The Stanford Cardinal in 1892 and 1894-1895.

He compiled during his amazing career an astounding record of 79 wins, 5 losses, and 3 ties, a winning percentage of 94 (if ties count as wins) or 87 (if ties count as losses). His teams in 1888, 1891, and 1892 were recognized by sports writers and fans as national champions.

Camp was truly a pioneer who introduced changes from rules adopted from Rugby that were imported from England, many of them to protect players from injury or worse and/or to accelerate play to be more enjoyable for spectators. At a rules convention in 1880, he introduced the line of scrimmage to eliminate rugby's dangerous scrum. In ensuing years, he introduced downs, the center snap, the safety, and new rules for scoring:

The game shall be decided by the final score at the end of the two halves. The following shall be the value of plays in scoring:

Touchdown: 6 points

Goal from touchdown: 1 point

Goal from the field: 3 points

Safety by opponents: 2 points

Walter displayed many diverse talents and ambitions. In addition to his contributions to American football, he worked himself up to Chairperson of the New Haven Clock Company, a family business, and wrote some 30 books and more than 250 magazine articles. He edited several sports books published by the Spalding Athletic Library.

I asked him to write a regular column for this newspaper. He politely declined, pleading that he was too busy. I understand.

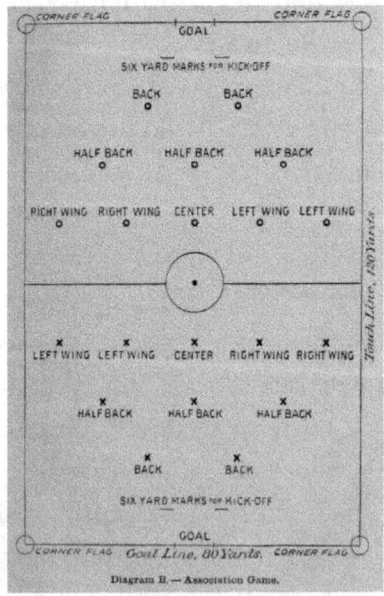

Walter Camp's book "American Football", 1891

Allegheny City, Pennsylvania   June 15, 1896

The death of AAA. We'll miss you.

By Sarah Scrivener

I am sad to report that our local football team, the Allegheny Athletic Association—which we all came to know as 'The Three A's'—has folded only 6 years after its founding. We thank the General Managers, OD Thompson, who served in 1890-1891 and 1893-1896, and Billy Kountz, who took over in 1892 when OD devoted his time and talents to playing. We also thank the head coach for all 6 years, Sport Donnelly.

The team gave all fans countless thrills while compiling a stellar record. This group of superb athletes won Western Pennsylvania championships in 1890, 1892, 1894, and 1896, when it was undefeated. Perhaps its most notable game when it defeated, in November 1892 of its cross-town rival, the Pittsburgh Athletic Club, 4-0, at our Recreation Park. The crowd of 500 rabid fans went wild when Pudge Heffelfinger—you may recall that he played for the Chicago Athletic Association and was paid $500 under the table to play one game for AAA—picked up a fumble and ran the ball 35 yards into the end zone for the game's only score. Pudge became an instant and admired hero in Allegheny City and an instant and despised cheat in the East End.

As you might expect but you weren't aware, PAC's General Manager, John Baxter Barbour, Jr. protested the win on the grounds that Pudge and 2 other players were paid professionals. OD retaliated by accusing the PAC of hiring Simon Martin, who was promised a paying job with PAC after the season ended. Both teams threatened to take their grievances to the Amateur Athletic Union but backed down when they realized that doing so might jeopardize their amateur status and erase their records.

For all you football fans: The Pittsburgh Athletic Club will play next season, at Recreation and Exposition Parks and others around the area, and the Alleghenys Baseball Club will be active this summer at Exposition Park. I'll be there and will report on its games as well as other events in our thriving city, just as I have for the past six years. Thanks for reading, and many thanks to all of you who called me an idiot (I'm being polite) for naming Louis Frederick Kirchner the first pro player when Pudge obviously earned that honor. I admit, I am biased toward players here on my home turf or nearby. Can you blame me?

There you are: I've settled the debate about naming the first pro football player. There was a plethora of candidates, so, still another heated debate is afoot, and I expect to take my rightful part. A Tom Boy like me can't resist a good fight. Ask any one of my seven brothers.

3.
BIRTHING BASEBALL AND THE TRENDSETTERS WHO MADE IT HAPPEN

My editor, Joe Siebeneck, and I are in love; our early baseball teams were pitiful but were saved by Honus Wagner, baseball's first super star, and dignitaries with deep pockets; like John Baxter Barbour, Jr.

November 10, 1896

I again met with my editor, Joseph Siebeneck at his home on Galveston to discuss my columns concerning sports in Allegheny City and Pittsburgh, and, occasionally, farther east in Latrobe and Greensburg and west to Cleveland and Chicago. I've become somewhat of a wanderer, wouldn't you say?

Joe suggested that I write one or two longer columns—each an entire page or two in the newspaper—concerning baseball. He reasoned, correctly it turns out, that the sport had been played in America since Colonial days and seemed to be gaining popularity with the public. He explained:

"Baseball is a far different sport than football (as if I didn't know, with my history of stickball on the streets of New York). It demands lightning-quick eye-hand coordination and the reflexes of a finely tuned cat, while football demands more heft and physical strength, not to mention the ability to endure pain."

"We in Allegheny City are blessed with an exciting baseball club owned by dedicated sportsmen and financiers with the resources to support the team through thick and thin. We also are blessed with two fine arenas in Recreation and Exposition Parks down by the Allegheny River, and a roster of colorful players with names such as Peek-a-Boo and Chappy and Pud. I remember Pud well. Back in 1877, only 19 years ago, I watched him pitch a shutout and hit a home run against the Boston Red Stockings. He won the game, 1-0, single-handedly."

"And I remember back in 1882 when George Strife—or is it Stief?—hit the first home run in the club's short history. Astounding when we consider that he hit only five four baggers during his entire career as a pro baseball player. He did hit four triples in one game, a record that stood for several years. Both Pud and George are sure to go down in history as among the finest athletes who played in Allegheny City, perhaps in all of America."

Mr. Siebeneck added that the sport was called 'town ball' or 'one old cat' for unknown reasons that might make an intriguing story. He suggested that I might start researching the local game by interviewing Palmer O'Neill, the president of the local team, the Alleghenys, and his side kick and part owner William Nimick. Other interesting interviewees include John Barbour, a founder of the Federal League of Baseball Clubs and a charter member of the Pittsburgh Athletic Club. Barbour is a wealthy oil broker and could very well be the money behind our local baseball and football clubs. I agreed, and started to write the first of my longer columns that I envisioned will come together as a book as soon as I can find the time. Here's my first column:

Sketch of Receation Park, 1894

Allegheny City, Pennsylvania December 12, 1896

Who Invented Baseball? It Depends.

By Sarah Scrivener, Senior Reporter

Dear readers, please indulge my curiosity. I decided to initiate my columns on baseball by studying its history and was enlightened and amused, as I hope you will be. It seems that men and boys—and girls too, I would imagine since I qualify, have been hitting a ball or rock with a stick since about 2400 BC, as evidenced by images on temple walls in ancient Egypt. Jump to 1744 England, when *A Little Pretty Pocket Book* published this poem:

Base-Ball

The ball once struck off.
 Away flies the Boy.

To the next destin'd post

And then Home with joy.

The poem is the first known mention of baseball in print, and it was likely a mistake. The writer probably had the game *rounders* in mind, a popular ancestor of modern baseball. He, or she, described rounders as a striking and fielding game during which a player hits a small, hard, leather-cased ball with a round wood or metal bat, then running around (hence the name) four bases to score. Sounds like baseball to me.

A Little Pretty Pocket Book is generally considered the first children's book and consists of simple rhymes for each letter of the alphabet. The publisher's marketing plan was simple and clever: the book came with either a ball for a boy, or a pincushion for a girl, a clear case of gender discrimination. The book was re-published in Colonial America in 1762, 134 years ago as I pen this. I wonder if Ben Franklin was involved.

He might have been. He was quite interested in promoting publishing and the language, and he was only 56 years old at the time. He was an excellent swimmer who grew stout as he aged, perhaps because he suffered from bladder stones that might have prevented him from strenuously exercising, but not from eating and drinking. He was known for his insatiable cravings for food and drink, and for saying, "God made beer because he loves us and wants us to be happy."

*

Ben's s kite and key to demonstrate electricity and its power is well known and lightning almost killed him. Less well known—he may be the first to barbecue. He cooked a turkey outdoors using electricity for a group of friends. We can be sure that beer was on the menu.

*

We will never know if Ben had his hand and printing presses in *A Little Pretty Pocket Book*. Nevertheless, we do know that we can thank our friends the British for inventing many stick-and-ball games, including cricket and rounders.

As I mentioned in an earlier column, my editor suggested that baseball may have its roots as *Own Ball, Town Ball,* or *Old Cat*. I found that it did.

Town ball was played in North America in the 18th and 19th centuries. It was similar to rounders and was a precursor to baseball In some areas such as Philadelphia and towns along the Ohio and Mississippi Rivers. In other regions the local game was named *base, baseball,* or just *ball.*

The "New York game" emerged in the 1840s it was sometimes dubbed the "New England game" or "Massachusetts baseball". The players might be schoolchildren or men in organized clubs in a pasture playing with improvised balls—a rock?—and bats—sticks?

As baseball became popular, town ball became a casual term to describe old fashioned or rural games similar to baseball.

One old cat continues to be commonly played in America. *One eyed cat,* or one-o'-cat was the basic version of the game, with a pitcher or giver; a batter or striker; a catcher, and sometimes another fielder or two. The striker, upon hitting the ball thrown by the giver, attempted to run to a single base (often the giver's position) and back again. The fielders tried to throw the ball to hit the striker/runner while they were not touching the base.

Strikers would also be out if the struck ball were caught in the air, or if they swung and missed three times at the giver's deliveries.

The Egyptians, Colonial

Americans, and the British all can legitimately claim to have invented baseball, and I thank them for their contributions to developing the game that we love so dearly. Other more contemporary contenders include:

Albert Spalding

(September 2, 1849 - September 9, 1915) could be the father of baseball (and future purveyor of sporting goods) for his lifelong participation in so many aspects of the game. He was a pitcher in the major leagues from 1871 through 1878. In 1871, Spalding joined the Boston Red Stockings and was highly successful; winning 206 games and losing only 53 as a pitcher and batting .323 as a hitter. He was among the early players—not the first—to wear a glove, a fingerless design that protected a player's palms from the sting of impact with a hard ball made of a rubber core wrapped in leather.

Doug Allison, a catcher for the Boston Red Stockings in the early 1870s, was the first player to wear a glove. He was followed by Charles Waitt, a first baseman for the Saint Louis Brown Stockings. Gloves were rare until 1877, when Spalding, by then a respected first baseman for the Chicago White Stockings, copied Waitt. To protect his catching hand. Players had worn gloves previously, but they were not popular; they were a sign of weakness—tough guys did not wear them. Spalding himself was skeptical of wearing one at first. However, once he began donning gloves, he realized their benefits and influenced other players to follow his example.

Spalding was dubbed *The premier pitcher of the 1870s*, leading the National league in victories for each of his six full seasons as a professional. He was his team's only pitcher for some seasons. In 1876, Spalding won 47 games as the prime pitcher for the White Stockings and led them to win the first-ever National League pennant by a wide margin.

After his retirement as a player in 1878, at age 27, Spalding remained active with the Chicago White Stockings as president and part-owner. In the 1880s, he took players on the first world tour of baseball. With William Hulbert, Spalding organized the National League. He later called for the commission that investigated the origins of baseball and falsely credited Abner Doubleday with creating the game.

Spalding's .796 career winning percentage (when teams played once or twice a week) is the highest ever by a baseball pitcher, .058 ahead of Negro league star Dave Brown's .738. Spalding was the first pitcher to win 200 games.

*

Because at the time African Americans were not accepted by organized baseball, African Americans formed their own teams and league. Pittsburgh was home to two of the more dominant teams, The Pittsburgh Crawfords and Homestead Grays. Josh Gibson, considered to be one of the best players ever, played for the Grays.

Before the 1870s players caught the ball with their cupped bare hands, then with the unpadded fingerless glove, followed by a padded glove with fingers, followed in the 1920s by a padded glove with flexible webbing between the first finger and thumb. It was conceived by Bill Doak, a pitcher for the Saint Louis Cardinals who became 'The Father of the modern baseball glove'. Doak's design evolved into several designs for specific positions. Infielders wear a glove with a shallow pocket for rapid retrieval of caught balls, outfielders wear gloves with deeper pockets and longer fingers, pitchers with tight webbing to hide the ball from batters, first basemen a glove with a thumb but no fingers. And catchers a glove with extra padding to absorb repeated impacts of thrown balls.

*

Henry Chadwick

(October 5, 1824 – April 20, 1908) has been dubbed *The Father of Baseball*. For his early reporting on the games and contributions to developing its rules. Henry was a sportswriter, baseball statistician and historian, He edited the first baseball guide that was sold to the public. He is credited with creating box scores, batting and earned run averages, and *K* to designate a strikeout.

Chadwick was one of the prime movers in the rise of baseball's popularity in the 1800s. A keen amateur statistician and professional writer, he helped shape the public perception of the game, as well as providing the basis for the records of teams' and players' achievements in the form of statistics. He also served on baseball rules committees and influenced how the game was played.

Chadwick could easily be dubbed *The Father of Sports Journalism*. He edited *The Beadle Dime Base-Ball Player*, the first annual baseball guide on public sale, and the Spalding and Reach annual guides. His 1861 *Beadle* listed totals of games played, outs, runs, home runs, and strikeouts for hitters on prominent clubs, the first database of its kind. His goal was to provide numerical evidence of which players helped a team to win.

Despite a close friendship with Albert Spalding, Chadwick scorned Spalding's attempts to declare Abner Doubleday the inventor of baseball. "He means well", said Chadwick, "but he doesn't know". Chadwick bequeathed to Spalding his extensive baseball library.

I think that **Alexander Cartwright**

(April 17, 1819 - July 12, 1892) is more deserving of being the inventor of baseball. He was a founder of the Knickerbocker Baseball Club in New York City. In 1845, he wrote the rules his club followed, and which were later adopted by other clubs in New York and Massachusetts. They now could play each other on equal footings, which encouraged attendance, honest debates, and gambling.

I read the rules and found them to be reasonable and still

applicable to our modern game except one. Initially, a ball hit out of the field was a foul; today it is a home run.

Despite the evidence favoring Cartwright as the inventor, he is over-shadowed by **Abner Doubleday**

(June 26, 1819 - January 26, 1893). He achieved minor fame as a competent combat general with roles in many important Civil War battles, including those at Fort Sumpter and Gettysburg. He is more widely known as the inventor of baseball who scratched out a rudimentary field in the dirt in a cow pasture or corn field in 1839, more than two decades before The Civil War, when Abner was twenty years old and a first-year cadet at West Point.

Realizing that the corn field story is fiction, in 1905 a committee of sports lovers and financiers, chaired by Abraham G. Mills, the fourth president of the National League, was appointed to determine the real origin of baseball. Some two years later, on December 30, 1907, the committee reported, in part, that, "the first scheme for playing baseball, according to the best evidence obtainable to date, was devised by Abner Doubleday at Cooperstown, New York, in 1839."

It concluded by noting, quite correctly, "in the years to come, in the view of the hundreds of thousands of people who are devoted to baseball, and the millions who will be, Abner Doubleday's fame will rest evenly, if not quite as much, upon the fact that he was its inventor ... as upon his brilliant and distinguished career as an officer in the Federal Army."

The conclusions of the Mills Commission are bogus, and fans and scholars have debunked the Doubleday-Cooperstown connection as a harmless myth. It nonetheless remains a powerful truth in the American imagination because Major League Baseball and the Hall of Fame in Cooperstown say so.

At his death, Doubleday left many letters and papers, none of which describe baseball or give any suggestion that he considered himself a prominent influence on the game's evolution. His New York Times obituary did not mention the game at all. Chairman Mills himself, who had been a Civil War colleague of Doubleday and a member of the honor guard for Doubleday's body as it lay in state in New York City, never recalled hearing Doubleday describe his role as the inventor.

There is more evidence that Abner could not have invented the game. Doubleday's family had moved away from Cooperstown the year before Abner allegedly scratched the dirt in a corn field.

Despite the lack of solid evidence linking Doubleday to the origins of baseball, Cooperstown, New York, became the new home of the *National Baseball Hall of Fame and Museum* in 1937.

*

On Feb 2, 1876, in Manhattan, a committee of sports lovers and investors founded The National League, replacing the failed National Association of Professional Base Ball Players. In 1901, Ban Johnson, president of the Westen League, formed The American League to exploit the National League's downsizing from 12 to 8 teams. Ban and his investors then raided players from The National League, including such Boston stars as Cy Young and Jimmy Collins, inciting owners of national league teams to block games pitting the winners of each league. Realizing the commercial windfall of such games, Johnson convinced Barney Dreyfuss, owner of the Pirates, to play an exhibition series against a team of American League All Stars.

The leagues resolved their disputes in the winter of 1902, and created a bipartisan National Commission to preside over organized baseball and to initiate the 1903 World Series.

*

Barney Dreyfuss (February 23, 1865 - February 5, 1932) owned the Pittsburgh Pirates from 1900 to his death. He is credited with initiating the first World Series and overseeing construction of the first steel and concrete stadium, Forbes Field, completed in Pittsburgh's Oakland neighborhood in 1909. During his tenure as owner, The Pirates won six National League titles, four fewer than the New York Giants won during the same 32 years, and the 1909 and 1925 World Series.

*

Barney Dreyfuss at exposition Park 1903

Allegheny City, Pennsylvania February 15, 1897

The Leagues Emerge From The Depths of Chaos

By Sarah Scrivener, Senior Reporter

I met with J. Palmer O'Neil (September 30, 1843 - January 6, 1908) president of the Alleghenys baseball Club and one of our many outstanding civic leaders. O'Neil worked for years as a life insurance executive in New York City and Pittsburgh, followed by a stint as a manufacturer of guns and hunting supplies. He helped to financially guide the Alleghenys team through its wretched 1890 season, when the club lost an unbelievable 113 games, a Major League record, while winning only 23. The team finished in last place, 66.5 games behind the Brooklyn Bridegrooms.

Our team can be forgiven for its wretched performance. They

faced stiff competition from the upstart Players League team, the Pittsburgh Burghers. Its roster boasted several outstanding players who had jumped from the Allegheny's, among them established stars pitcher Pud Galvin, first baseman Jake Beckley, and outfielder Ned Hanlon (aka Foxy Ned) who also served as the team's manager.

*

Meanwhile, John Tener, who would go on to represent Pittsburgh in the United States Congress and be elected the 25th Governor of Pennsylvania, finished his pitching career with the Burghers in 1890. Later, Tener would become the president of the National League, and a director of the Philadelphia Phillies.

*

In their only season, the Burghers, who played at the Alleghenys' former home, Exposition Park, finished in sixth place with a 60–68 record. First baseman Jake Beckley was a bright spot. He hit .324 with 10 home runs and 120 RBIs, and he led the league with 22 triples. But even Beckley's exceptional performance could not overcome the team's weak hitting. The Burghers finished tied for the league's worst batting average, a woeful .260.

I asked Palmer to tell me about the disastrous 1890 season:

"We had been in the National League for only three years, since 1887, when Recreation Park was our home field. It is bounded by Allegheny, Pennsylvania, Grant, (now Galveston, where your editor lives) Avenues, and Bouquet (now Behan) Street. Recreation Park has been known at various times over the years as Union Park, 3A Park, and the Coliseum. It was a sporting grounds and stadium that stood from 1865 to 1905, forty active years

The field was our first home as National Leaguers. It was also home to many football games played by The Western University of Pittsburgh and, in November 1892, the first American football game that allegedly fielded a professional player.

Opened in 1865 as a skating center, Recreation Park was adapted for baseball in 1867. Known until 1885 as Union Park, the stadium had an early capacity of 2,500 and was later expanded with wooden grandstands to allow up to 17,000 spectators. After the Alleghenys moved a few blocks south in 1890, the main tenant became the Allegheny Athletic Association, and the grounds would eventually be referred to as 3A Park. After the turn of the 20th century, it was converted to a velodrome, complete with a track for cycling. It was called *The Coliseum*.

In the late 1860s and early 70s, Pittsburgh was home to three local amateur baseball teams—the Enterprise Club, the Xanthas, and the Olympics—which played most of their games in Union Park. In 1876, the Alleghenys played its first game against Xantha at Union Park, winning 7-3.

The Alleghenys lasted for three years, playing mostly other squads from the northeast within the International Association, but occasionally taking on National League teams in exhibition games. One long-remembered match took place in early May 1877, when Pud Galvin threw a shutout and hit a home run in a 0-1 victory over the Boston Red Stockings. In 1884, the two-year-old Pittsburgh Alleghenys of the American Association won 18 games and lost 17, finishing 11th in the league.

The ballpark was used as a neutral site for one game in

the 1885 World Series and for one game in the 1887 World Series.

In 1887, part owner William A. Nimick transferred the club into the National League, and on April 30, the Alleghenys defeated the Chicago White Stockings, 6–2 in front of 10,000 spectators, the first officially recognized contest of the Pittsburgh Pirates franchise.

Legend has it that, before the opening game of the 1887 season, Pittsburgh's catcher Fred Carroll buried his pet monkey beneath home plate, ostensibly to bring good luck and more wins to the team. Also, during that season, local businessman Walter Brown organized a league for African American ballplayers, with his Pittsburgh Keystones taking up residence at the park. In 1891, after the collapse of the Pittsburgh Burghers, the Alleghenys moved to the third incarnation of Exposition Park, which had been constructed for the Burghers.

*

In 1902, a Pirates-backed football team, the Pittsburgh Stars of the first National Football League, played its home games at the field. The Stars would win the league's only championship, against the Philadelphia Athletics.

The Western University of Pittsburgh (WUP) football team played their first game of the 1898 season at Recreation Park, defeating Westminster 0–5.

*

Eighteen ninety was our ninth season and it was awful, discouraging for the owner, Bill Nimick, and our manager, Guy Hecker, who I'm sure you will want to meet as part of your reporting. We lost 113 games, won only 23, and ended the season dead last in The National League, 66.5 games behind the Brooklyn Bridegrooms. They won 86 games and lost only 43. Embarrassing for us, eh?

We set a new major league record for losses, breaking the old record of 111 set last year—the 1889 season—by the Louisville Colonels.

I do not like to make excuses for why we were so pathetic that year, but we have one of our own doings. Most of our better players defected to our local rivals, The Pittsburgh Burghers, for more money and, I think, for higher hopes of playing more seasons with a more established club. I'm only guessing.

The next year, 1891, The Alleghenys became the Pittsburgh Pirates and competed in the National League. Bill Nimick was president during those years and was one of four owners as well. He sold his shares to William Chase Temple following the 1891 season.

The Pittsburg national league base ball club, 1890

Allegheny City, Pennsylvania								June, 1903

Hey Allegheny City: It's Time To Celebrate Our Past.

By Sarah Scrivener, Senior Reporter

5th Ave. west from Smithfield, Pittsburgh, PA, 1903

We have an illustrious past and it is time to tell the world. A few examples:

Our Alleghenys baseball team set two historic firsts in n 1877. On June 2 they played the first game decided in 19 innings, defeated by a club representing Memphis, Tennessee. On June 20 that same year, The Alleghenys tied a club representing Indianapolis in 17 innings.

Allegheny City spawned more than sports. It is also a hub for engineering that improves lives and lifestyles and is personified by George Ferris and George Westinghouse. The Columbian EXPO would still be on the drawing boards if it were not for them.

The Ferris Wheel was surely the main attraction of the EXPO that was filled with amazing buildings and technologies. The wheel's inventor, George Ferris, lived with his wife Margaret on Arch Street for three years. He had already conceived of a vertical wheel that would carry people to unimagined heights when he was young in Nevada and was fascinated by the water wheels that irrigated the ranch on which he and his family lived.

After graduating from Rensselaer Polytechnic Institute, one of America's top engineering schools, with a degree in Civil Engineering, he supervised the construction of bridges in West Virginia and Pennsylvania. He then formed an engineering company that specialized in testing the properties of that new material, steel, with headquarters on Grant Street in downtown Pittsburgh. He commuted there from Allegheny City every day until he and Margaret moved there for larger quarters and to be closer to George's thriving business.

His company prospered and was awarded a contract to test materials used to build the EXPO. At a luncheon in Chicago, he and other engineers were challenged to design and build an icon that would outshine The Eiffel Tower in Paris. He conceived his Wheel—an innovative design that changed architecture and structural engineering forever as well as the way we amuse ourselves. Today, ten years later, hundreds of Ferris Wheels dot the skylines of cities around the world, p most notably the Prater in Vienna, Austria that was completed in 1897 and is still operating.

The Wiener Riesenrad, or simply The Prater Ferris Wheel, is 64.75-metres (212 ft) high located at the entrance of the Prater amusement park in Vienna. It was designed by British engineers using principles conceived and refined in Allegheny City by George Ferris and William Gronau and constructed in 1897 by another

British engineer. Its purpose was to celebrate the *Golden Jubilee* of Emperor Franz Joseph I. it was one of the earliest Ferris wheels built after the EXPO closed and its wheel scrapped in St. Louis in the early 1900s.

George Ferris was treated shabbily by Daniel Burnham, the chief architect and manager for the largest construction project in America at the time. George became depressed and contracted Typhoid fever. He died in Pittsburgh's Mercy Hospital at age 37, a broken man. A pity. I think he will be the most famous engineer from this area. Millions will know his name on the wheel, but they will not know the man.

George Westinghouse added: "Many of my colleagues and friends think of me as an accomplished engineer and businessman. I think of myself as a tinkerer turned engineer without a minute of formal training, and a novice businessman. I delegate much of my business activities to my brother Herman, who is a more astute financier and visionary than I can ever be. My colleagues—bless them—tell me that I influenced the success of The EXPO as much as George Ferris did. My light bulbs—thousands of them—were a modern design that outperformed and outlasted the bulbs offered by Thomas Edison. I am proud of that."

The Prater Ferris Wheel as painted by Henry Koerner, a Pittsburgh artist. The paining is a valued part of the author's gallery only a short distance from George Ferris's home.

Allegheny City, Pennsylvania	September 15, 1903

Let's Start A New Tradition: Naming The Most Valuable Alleghenys Player.

By Sarah Scrivener, Senior Reporter

Not an easy task, naming an MVP, but I tried, first by examining game statistics and fan appeal, which is mostly opinion. I narrowed the field of hundreds of players to the few who were or are the most valuable to the team, its fans, and our growing city.

I decided that the most valuable pitcher is **Frank Bissell "Lefty" Killen**

(November 30, 1870 - December 3, 1939) a stellar southpaw during parts of ten seasons (1891–1900) with the Milwaukee Brewers, Washington Senators, Boston Beaneaters, Chicago Orphans, and our Alleghenys, where he stayed for five seasons.

In 1893, Killen posted a league-best 36 victories against 14 defeats. No left-hander in league history has won as many. He was the league's best in 1893 and 1896. In 1896, for example, he led the league in complete games and shutouts.

He was remarkably durable and versatile: He won 164 games while losing only 131 in 321 appearances, with a 3.78 ERA and 725 strikeouts. As a hitter, Killen posted a career .241 batting average with 11 home runs, 127 RBIs, and 151 runs scored. He also drew

131 bases on balls with his sharp eye for strikes.

His playing days over, Killen returned to live quietly in the neighborhood in Allegheny City in which he grew up, the *Mexican War Streets*, originally known as the *Buena Vista Tract*. The district is densely filled with restored row houses, community gardens, and tree-lined streets and alleyways.

The area dates to around the time of the Mexican American War (1846—1848) It was developed from land owned by William Robinson Jr., an ex-mayor of the city of Allegheny who was in office from July 1840 to January 1841. He subdivided the property into streets and lots in 1847. Alexander Hays surveyed the property for development.

Several of the streets are named after battles and generals of the Mexican–American War, including Buena Vista Street, Monterey Street, Palo Alto Street, Resaca Place (Killen's early address), Sherman Avenue, and Taylor Avenue. Fremont Street is an exception: it was named for John C. Frémont, an officer in The Civil War.

Pud Galvin's

(December 25, 1856 - March 7, 1902) performance as a pitcher and hitter is as remarkable as Killen's. He was the Major League's first 300-game winner and a fine hitter: I n 1877, Pud pitched a shutout and hit a home run against the Boston Red Stockings, winning the game almost single-handedly.

He pitched for the Alleghenys when they were in the American Association, for the Pirates when they joined the National League, and the Pittsburgh Burghers of the Players League.

In his first full season in the major leagues, 1879, Galvin won 37 games and lost 27 with a 2.28 earned run average. On August 20, 1880, he became the first major league pitcher to throw a no-hitter on the road, leading his Buffalo Bisons to a 0–1 victory over the Worcester Worcesters. He pitched over 400 innings in 1880, 1881, and 1882. In 1883, Galvin went 46–29 with a 2.72 ERA, setting career highs in wins, games started (75), complete games (72), and innings pitched (656.1); he led the national League in the latter three categories. The following season, in 1884, he went 46–22 with a remarkable 1.99 ERA in 72 games started, 71 complete games, and 636.1 innings pitched.

Galvin was traded to the Pittsburgh Alleghenys midseason in 1885. He played for the Alleghenys club from 1885 to 1889, pitching over 300 innings each year. He jumped to the Pittsburgh Burghers of the short-lived Players League before the 1890 season and then returned to the Alleghenys (now named the *Pirates*) after the season.

The nickname *Pud* originated because Galvin was said to make hitters 'look like pudding.' Galvin was also nicknamed "The Little Steam Engine", a tribute to his power despite his small size. He was sometimes known as "Gentle Jeems" because of his kind disposition.

Deacon Phillippe

(May 23, 1872 - March 30, 1952) Is on my list of Most Valuable by winning three of the five complete games he pitched in the 1903 World Series. In the first game he struck out ten Boston batters, a herculean feat. Not to be outdone, the next day Boston pitcher Bill Dinneen struck out eleven Pittsburgh batters.

Fred Clifford Clarke

(October 3, 1872 - August 14 1960), Left fielder, joined the major leagues in 1894 and became a player/manager soon after. He throws and bats left-handed. Before joining the Alleghenys he played for and managed the Louisville Colonels and other major league teams.

Clarke was the player-manager for four of the nine pennants in Pittsburgh franchise history. He, Honus Wagner, and Vic Willis led Pittsburgh to a victory over Ty Cobb and the Detroit Tigers in the 1909 World Series.

Clarke batted over .300 in 11 different seasons, his 35-game hitting streak in 1895 was the second-longest in Major League history. For six years, Clarke held the Major League record for wins by a manager.

In his first game in the majors, Clarke collected five hits in five at bats, a record. In his second season, his batting average of .347, 191 hits and 96 runs, were all best on the team by far. In 1897, Clark became manager when only 24 years old.

As a player, he hit a career-high .390. Only the best average of Willie Keeler's career stopped Clarke from winning his only batting title.

In 1900, Clarke joined the Pittsburgh Pirates as a player and manager. In 1903, he led the Major Leagues in slugging average, the National League in doubles. He finished second only to his teammate, Honus Wagner, for the National League batting title. Clarke hit .265. in the first World Series.

Clarke batted only .211 In the 1909 World Series, but hit both of Pittsburgh's home runs and had more home runs and RBIs than any player on either team. Clarke walked four times in game 7, a record.

*

1903 was a year of wild successes for Allegheny City and its athletes, engineers and ordinary citizens. In sports it marked the first Modern World Series (but not the first World Series). In the 1885 World Series, the National League champion Chicago White Stockings faced the American Association champion St. Louis Browns. The series, played in Chicago, St. Louis, Pittsburgh, and Cincinnati, ended in a disputed 3-3-1 tie. In 1887, the Detroit Wolverines of the National League defeated the St. Louis Browns 10 games to 5 in the World Series, played from October 10 to 26 in various cities, including Detroit and St. Louis. Detroit clinched the series in game 11. It also marked the first Ferris Wheel. All of America, and, in fact all the world, reveled in its grandeur, and George Ferris was extolled as an engineering genius. A month later a builder of a smaller wooden vertical wheel sued George for patent infringement. Legal and other fees bankrupted George and he died only a few years later in a Pittsburgh hospital.

1903 was sad for America. Tom Edison, in his misdirected zeal to prove that George Westinghouse's alternating current electricity (AC) is more dangerous than his direct current (DC) ordered several of his technicians to electrocute Topsy, an innocent circus elephant. The horrendous act of cruelty accelerated America's first Standards War, which AC won. Edison admitted later in life that he was wrong.

*

George Strife (aka Strief)

(October 16, 1856 – April 1, 1946), the team's second baseman, hit the first home run for the Alleghenys, on May 3, 1882, against the Cincinnati Red Stockings in a 7-3 loss.

In 1885, Strife set the record for most triples in a game, four, tied by Bill Joyce in 1897, and was the first player to collect five extra base hits in a game.

Johannes Peter "Honus" Wagner

(February 24, 1874-December 6, 1955), is sometimes referred to as Hans Wagner. A brilliant shortstop, he is destined to play many more seasons and will be enshrined as one of the most valuable players of all time. Wagner was nicknamed "the Flying Dutchman" due to his superb speed and German heritage.

*

This nickname was a nod to the popular folk tale made into a musical drama, aka opera, by the German composer and namesake, Richard Wagner. It was first performed in Dresden in 1843. Its plot revolved around a curse that condemned The Dutchman to a lifetime of wandering until he finds a woman who will swear to be faithful.

*

Allegheny City, Pennsylvania   October 1903

The First World Series? Or Another Myth?

By Sarah Scrivener, Senior Reporter

In 1903, the Pirates played the Boston Americans in, allegedly, Major League Baseball's inaugural World Series. Wagner, by this point, was an established star and much was expected of him, especially since the Pirates' starting roster was decimated by injury.

Wagner himself was not at full strength and hit only .222 for the series. The Americans, meanwhile, had some fans, called the "Royal Rooters" who, whenever Wagner came to bat, sang "Honus, Honus, why do you hit so badly?" To the tune of "Tessie", a popular song of the day. The Rooters, led by Boston bartender Michael "Nuf Ced" McGreevy, even traveled to Pittsburgh to continue their heckling.

Pittsburgh lost the best-of-nine series, five games to three, to a team led by pitchers Cy Young and Bill Dinneen, and third baseman/manager Jimmy Collins. Christy Mathewson, in his book 'Pitching in a Pinch' wrote: "For some time after Wagner's poor showing in the World Series of 1903 ... it was reported that he was yellow, the real tragedy in Wagner's career. Notwithstanding his stolid appearance, he is a sensitive player, and this has hurt him more than anything else in his life ever has."

Wagner was disturbed by his performance. The following spring, he refused to send his portrait to a Hall of Fame for batting champions, citing his play in the World Series. "I was too bum last year", he wrote. "I was a joke in that Boston-Pittsburgh Series. What does it profit a man to hammer along and make a few hits when they are not needed only to fall down when it comes to a pinch? I would be ashamed to have my picture up now."

Wagner and the Pirates proved that they were not yellow in the 1909 World Series, when the Pirates defeated The Tigers in seven games.

Wagner went on to collect eight batting titles while playing for 21 seasons, all with the Aleghenys and its successor, The Pittsburgh Pirates.

*

Conventional wisdom—and a historical marker directly across the Allegheny River on Pittsburgh's North Shore—dictates that the modern World Series began in 1903. It became an annual event in 1905. Before 1882, there were no playoff rounds—all championships went to the team with the best record at the end of the season. That system worked well until 1876, the initial season of the National League, when naming the champion ignited fierce debate: Was it the Chicago White Stockings, who had the best overall record (52–14), or the St. Louis Brown Stockings (19–45), the only team with a winning record against every other franchise in the league.

The teams agreed to play a five-game "Championship of the West" series. St. Louis prevailed, four games to one.

Was that a World Series?

The players of the 1903 World Series: The Pirates: (Top, left to right) - second baseman Claude Ritchey, catcher Harry Smith, catcher Eddie Phelps, outfielder Ginger Beaumont, pitcher Deacon Phillippe, pitcher Sam Leever, pitcher Bucky Veil, pitcher Gus Thompson, outfielder Tommy Leach, outfielder Jimmy Sebring, pitcher Brickyard Kennedy, catcher Fred Carisch and shortstop Honus Wagner.

Middle: Pirate manager and outfielder Fred Clarke. Boston players: third baseman-manager Jimmie Collins, outfielder Chick Stahl, pitcher Bill Dineen, outfielder Buck Freeman, pitcher Cy Young, first baseman Candy LaChance, outfielder Patsy Dougherty, pitcher George Winter, catcher Duke Farrell, outfielder Jack O'Brien, pitcher Long Tom Hughes.

Bottom: shortstop Fred Parent, catcher Lou Criger, second baseman Hobe Ferris

4.
THE FUTURE OF ORGANIZED SPORTS: IS MY VISION YOURS?

Sarah denounces violence but praises sports as a source of pleasure for the citizens of The Phantom City, America, and the World.

Perhaps as a woman I am a bit squeamish and denounce violence at all costs, but as a lover of the games I admire the skills displayed on the fields of battle by superb athletes. That said, rest assured that I am fully aware that football is violent and may cause more harm than good. I abhor that aspect of the game.

Players risk life and significant injury every moment they are on the field despite protective padding and rules of safe conduct written by Walter Camp that are enforced by at least three referees, and despite being endorsed by our sadistic president of America, Teddy Roosevelt. Anybody who can shoot elephants and other big game cannot care a twit about a few lost teeth, bloody noses, and broken jaws. Are deaths another matter?

Does Teddy, he of the bully pulpit, know that in 1905, the very middle of his presidency, nineteen players, all college students, died while playing football, sparking widespread calls for banning the game. It didn't happen and is not happening; the lure of violence is so great. Are we no better than the Greeks and Romans watching gladiators kill each other? Is football another deadly spectacle?

Baseball is of course not violent—yes, I know that players can collide when sliding into a base or looking up while chasing a fly ball—but otherwise it isn't violent when played within the rules, so to many fans it is boring, and boredom was and is the reason for sports in the first place.

*

The key words are *"played within the rules"*, *the perilous responsibility of umpires who, in the late 1800s often suffered violent abuse from players, fans, owners, and reporters. Although many baseball fans were disgusted by the turmoil, the owners failed to change the rules.*

"The pay is good, and you can't beat the hours," umpire Tim Hurst said, but in fact few men long endured umpiring for long. Half a season, a year, were routine tenures. Most umpires were hired sight unseen by National League president Nick Young, and many were ex-ballplayers with no experience. Young's failure to rotate umpires—one man commonly worked an entire home stand or more –allowed minor tiffs to escalate into running feuds, fist fights, and lifetime grudges.

One reporter noted: The time will soon come when no person above the rank of garrotter can be hired to umpire a game."

The obvious conclusion is that, if baseball is to survive as our national pastime (or even as our neighborhood frivolity) it must interject violence and/or speed—excitement—into the games, as have our Honus Wagner, Detroit's Ty Cobb, Boston's Cy Young, and Baltimore's Wee Willy Keeler.

I predict that football and baseball—in fact, other sports as well—will thrive for the near future and beyond, centuries at the very least. My reason: America is still growing and becoming more productive, creating leisure time for workers to fill with pleasurable pursuits, just as they did in the late 1800s. Also, women will be more involved. Colleges will field women's teams that play in women's leagues, as will handicapped and Black people regardless of gender or professional status.

'Inclusive' and 'survival' will be worthy goals that will remain elusive until organized sports adopt a comprehensive code of ethics that addresses the need for a higher level of sportsmanship for players, officials, owners, and fans on and off the playing field. I see three imperatives:

1) Equal treatment and fair play for all, which in turn requires knowledge and acceptance of the rules whether written or oral;

2) severe punishment for willfully harming another participant (A.S. Valentine's behavior will not be tolerated); and

3) significant rewards for helping others physically, fiscally, and emotionally whether they participate in the sport or not. I suggest public announcements such as newspaper headlines and editorials for participants who 'do the right thing', which will enhance public acceptance and perceptions, fill stadiums, and help sustain sports well into the future.

To explain further, the code should also stipulate that

1) All participants play within the rules—Walter Camp wrote them for football and Alex Cartwright for baseball to prevent injuries and encourage fair competition, in turn increasing the public's interest in the games and attendance.

2) Breaking the rules must be punished severely.

3) always respect the decisions of umpires even if you disagree with them.

4) Begin with the ending in mind; know the implications of actions, behave to enhance your life and the lives of others.

5) Act with integrity—recognize the need to be true to your own ethical/moral standards.

6) Practice what you advocate (walk the talk) and honestly admit discrepancies of thought and action.

7) Be truthful: Mendacity is always unethical; truth always respected.

Allegheny City, Pennsylvania   January 1904

Dignitaries Behind The Athletes, Some With Deep Pockets, All With A Deep Love For The Games

By Sarah Scrivener, Senior Reporter

John Baxter Barbour Jr.

(April 16, 1862 - March 11, 1929) was a wealthy investment banker/oil trader who was also a sports enthusiast. He was a founder of the Federal League of Baseball Clubs, and a charter member of The Pittsburgh Athletic Club (PAC) which he was instrumental in organizing in 1883. He then served three times as president and several seasons as manager of the baseball and football teams.

William Nimick

(September 2, 184 8- January 19, 1907) owned one-fourth of the Alleghenys and was president of the team during the 1885-1890 seasons. The team competed in the American Association from 1882-1886, and in the National League in 1887. He sold his shares after the 1891 season, when the team became the Pirates, to William Chase Temple, a coal, citrus, and lumber baron. Nimick died in Pasadena, California where he had moved for his health.

James G. Wyman

(1851 - 1910) was a four-time mayor of Allegheny City with a talent for winning elections despite his criminal record. Wyman served from 1884-1887, 1890-1892, 1899-1901, and 1903-1906. He frequently attended sporting events at Recreation and Exposition Parks and was a close friend and associate with Bill Nimick and other owners of the local teams.

In 1892, while serving in his second tenure, he was impeached for extortion and embezzlement, the only Mayor of Allegheny City to be criminally indicted. I do not know the details, and neither do any of the several of our leaders whom I asked. One guessed that he was caught skimming from the gate receipts collected at our popular sports events. More plausibly, he created an enemy or two, not unusual for ambitious politicians, and one of them charged Wyman with malfeasance under the aptly named ripper bill, a legislative bill or act for removing powers from the usual holders of these powers, then conferring them unrestrictedly on a chief executive, a governor or mayor, or on a board of officials. I know many of those officials and cannot imagine any of them resorting to such extreme, arbitrary actions, but obviously someone did. Regardless, impeachment did not prevent Mayor Wyman from being elected again in 1899 and 1903. Wyman died of pneumonia at age 59.

George Westinghouse

(October 6, 1846 - May 12, 1914), America's most influential and compassionate engineer/entrepreneur, built his first plant to design, make, and test his air brakes close to the site of Exposition Park on the banks of the Allegheny River. He later moved the plant to Wilmerding, a suburb only a few miles away. He is credited with electrifying America with Alternating current, not the Direct Current advocated by Thomas Edison.

George Ferris

(February 14, 1859 - November 22, 1896) is America's most unknown and famous engineer. No question: George Ferris was a creative, accomplished engineer, and, when he first lived in Allegheny City, he was thought of as an astute businessperson who could charm bankers and venture capitalists to finance his consulting businesses. He and his beautiful dark-haired wife Margaret were often seen at Exposition Park, a short walk from their home on Arch Street, enjoying football and baseball games.

In his later years, he lost his business sense and failed to patent his innovative design for the first Ferris wheel installed at the 1893 Columbian Exposition in Chicago. The result was thousands of copycat wheels built worldwide without paying George a penny and he died, broke, at age 37. His wheel soon became a visible part of the World's entertainment, competing with sports for the public's leisure time and excess cash.

The Ferris wheel at the 1893 Columbian Exposition in Chicago

May 15, 1910

Epilogue:

Sarah Speaks To The Graduating Class Of Western University Of Pennsylvania

 Good afternoon, and congratulations on earning your degree. It is your ticket to happiness, prosperity, and your chosen lifestyle. It is your ticket to a fulfilled and satisfying life. You are responsible for making that happen, and I know that you are up to the task.

 You couldn't have picked a better time. History has never witnessed an explosion of economic vigor like that in America during the three decades between 1880 and 1910, despite a painful downturn in the early 1890s.

Businesses are growing, led by steel, oil, food, railroads, and chemicals, and soon, I predict, aluminum and it's spin offs such as cookware and automobiles

Store shelves are bulging and sagging with new and tasty foodstuffs such as salad dressings, coca cola, Postum, Jello, and on and on. O, I forgot—Pabst, the beer that won a blue ribbon at the Chicago EXPO in 1893. I'm betting that many of you are familiar with it. Other beers such as Shaeffer's, when you're having more than one, and Schlitz, the beer that made Milwaukie famous are clamoring for awards, shelf space, and your dollars.

On the political front, I hear the first rumblings of women being allowed to vote. I say it's about time, and I've talked to President Taft of my leanings. He was receptive and I think will act in our and the nation's best interests.

The bottom line is that the world has never seen such an outpouring of goods and social change and it is not slowing or perish the thought, stopping. The world has also never been more receptive, more welcoming, of new, fresh minds full of creative ideas that improve the human condition.

My new Model T automobile—you might have noticed it in the parking lot, a new use of real estate that is replacing the hitching posts—is a *Lally-cooler*, proof of our nation's vigor. It was one of the first to come off the assembly line in Michigan; it is a marvel of design and manufacturing engineering. It will make our growing love affair with autos that was born a few years ago affordable for the average worker, and I predict that soon many families will own one or more.

Our popular sports, mainly football and baseball, need your help to reduce the number and severity of injuries and to be more accessible to working families.

Some suggestions: You who lean toward the law, examine the rules of football that were written by Walter Camp some fifty years ago. The game has changed since then to be more civil, more respectful of the well-being of players, so the rules surely need to change as well. You can write and enforce them.

You who lean toward protecting players to prevent injuries, redesign the uniforms to be less bulky, lightweight to be more comfortable, made of materials that can absorb more shock, are readily available and easily sewn so that uniforms can be made at home by understanding wives and mothers. The key word here is 'standardized' to thwart any unfair advantage.

While you are rewriting rules and redesigning uniforms to prevent injuries, do not forget the need to shorten the games. Most fans have limited free time, and it should not be wasted.

Some 15 years ago the dean of Syracuse University's School of Journalism asked me to speak at my own graduation. He asked if I could address the most important tools that enhanced my life and the lives of others that I had acquired during my four years there, in that idyllic spot in upstate New York. I came up with three of what I call my epiphanies: they are applicable to any profession or way of life.

The first is a deep respect for truth. I learned that telling a thumper is grounds for severe reprimand and that there are two or more sides to every story. Picking the one truth is a huge responsibility that can border on impossible. There is such a situation as true, less true, and truer. It's called compromise, judgement, or intuition. Journalists need to find and report it.

Just before I graduated from university, I accepted a position with Joseph Pulitzer's New York World as a Cub Reporter, a huge mistake that I perpetuated for almost five years. I did not know that Pulitzer and William Randolph Hearst would soon be battling over who could write the most sensational headlines and print the most sensational pictures and cartoons. All were lies, of course, violating my sense of ethics and the hard rule that mendacity is always wrong. I soon tired of apologizing for their misbehavior and resigned, an important reason I am here.

Which brings me to an important bit of advice, the only advice I will offer today. When considering employment, accept the offer from the more ethical firm and owner or manager. You'll know him by his smile that won't go away. You will be much happier too.

The second of my epiphanies is a deep respect for my fellow citizens. I will treat everybody with the dignity and ethical compass that they deserve. I expect to be treated in the same way. I will never knowingly harm anyone physically, fiscally, or emotionally. Instead, I will help anyone I can physically, fiscally, and emotionally.

The third is a deep respect for learning. Honestly, I can't stop reading good books that offer advice that improves my happiness, sense of well-being, and my finances. The library is my second home, the librarian and her books and knowledge are among my best and closest friends.

These three epiphanies have served me well financially and

emotionally during my tenure at Allegheny City, in fact all my life although I didn't know it. Allow me to illustrate.

When I arrived at the Allegheny City rail depot I was immediately welcomed warmly and respectfully by Mayor Wyman and the editor and owner of the local newspaper, Joseph Siebeneck. I've worked with him, and I know for sure that we have never hurt or lied to each other. I would not be standing here if we had.

My deep respect for learning led me to some fascinating facts about Allegheny City. Did you know that our resident engineers, businesspeople, and mayors spawned folk music, modern art, and political shenanigans worthy of a Hawthorne novel. For example:

Mayor William Barclay Foster, who served from 1842-1844, was the father of Stephen Foster. He gave me my fictional role model, Nellie Bly. Americans will be humming his tunes for centuries.

Mayor Robert Simpson Cassat was the father of painter Mary Cassat. Art lovers from around the world will be admiring her impressionist works for centuries.

Mayor Simon Drum, on Valentine's Day, 1861, greeted Abraham Lincoln while Honest Abe visited here, then resigned to fight in The Civil War. A true patriot.

Allegheny City also spawned creative engineering beyond imagination. George Westinghouse manufactured his first air brakes here, remarkably close to where we are at the moment. That one technological advance continues to save the lives of countless railroad brakemen. And William Gronea and George Ferris partnered to develop a new method for designing structures, enabling skyscrapers.

I have no doubts that you will carry on the traditions, and I will be here to witness it. Thank you.

Appendix 1

More About the Gilded Age,

the Gilded age is aptly named. It is a period of economic growth as the United States jumped to the lead in industrialization ahead of Great Britain. The nation was rapidly expanding its economy into new areas, especially heavy industries like steel, railroads, and coal mining. Prosperity was everywhere, perhaps most visible in ball parks, athletic clubs, and the mammoth EXPO in Chicago and St. Louis.

Other forms of entertainment such as fairs and traveling circuses (think P.T. Barnum, The Ringling Brothers, and countless others of lesser fame) grew concurrently, many spurred by the maturing of engineering, railroads, banking, and the ego-maniacal desire to show America's might to the world, a prime reason for the EXPO and Ferris Wheel. We became the Consumer Society with its efficient manufacturing and expanding leisure time long before it became fashionable and a global phenomenon.

Based solely on palpable optimism, much of it displayed at the EXPO and our bustling but horribly dirty and unhealthy cities, most of the millions of average, middle-income, hardworking Americans believed that their economic and political systems—their social order—were the world's best and wisest. For proof, they pointed to the growth of the country under freedom, the preservation of the nation after its disunion in 1861-1865, the abolition of slavery. Ransom Olds' and Henry Ford's first automobiles, George Westinghouse's breakthrough electricity generators at Niagara Falls, a vast network of railroads, and Gillette's new safety razors.

The nation—all of it—was surely fertile ground for the development and subsequent growth of organized sports, first played mostly by amateurs solely for the love of the game. Later—perhaps starting in the mid-1800s—sports were played increasingly by anonymous professionals, i.e., accomplished athletes who played for the love of the game and for pay, as little as it was, and to entertain themselves and their expanding horde of fans.

Other phenomena:

- The first transcontinental railroad opened the far-west mining and ranching regions.

- American steel production surpassed the combined totals of Britain, Germany, and France, and 60 percent of US steel was made in the Pittsburgh region.

- Investors in London and Paris poured money into the railroads through the American financial market centered in Wall Street and J.P. Morgan.

- A few large corporations, called "trusts", dominated steel, oil, sugar, meat, and farm machinery.

- Frederick Winslow Taylor observed that worker efficiency could be improved.

- The number of unskilled and skilled workers increased as their wage rates grew.

- Engineering colleges were established to feed the enormous demand for expertise.

- From 1860 to 1890, 30 years, 500,000 patents were issued for new inventions, more than ten times the number granted in the previous seventy years.

- Electric lights replaced gas lights, thanks to the genius of Tom Edison, Nikolai Tesla, and George Westinghouse.

Appendix 2

More About Your Author and FUN

Pete Geissler is the Willy Sutton of business. Willy was a famous bank robber who plied his trade in the early 1900s. Reporter Mitch Ohnstad supposedly asked Willy why he robbed banks. According to Ohnstad, Willy replied, "Because that's where the money is". The quote evolved into Sutton's Law, which is often invoked to medical students as a metaphor for emphasizing the most likely diagnosis, rather than wasting time and money investigating every conceivable possibility.

Willy offered another answer that was far less obvious: "Why did I rob banks? Because I enjoyed it. I loved it. I was more alive when I was inside a bank, robbing it, than at any other time in my life. I enjoyed everything about it so much that one or two weeks later I'd be out looking for the next job. Money is a bonus. Pete Geissler stole his three, contradictory laws for success from Willy:

Psychic Fit: Work diligently at whatever discipline you love; the money will follow.

Commitment Fit: Writing is demanding work; only a dunce would write for anything but unfettered love or money.

Location Fit: Serendipity is your friend; take advantage of it by being in the right places at the right times.

Pudge, Walter, Honus, Louis and other players chronicled herein knew and followed the three rules intuitively but had no clue that they were. They would have been successful at any endeavor except loafing.

Pete is a practicing writer and publisher of corporate gargle because that's where the money is. He and FUN are products of location. He has lived for decades in the heart of the former Allegheny City, where much of the action—the pathos, chicanery, subterfuge, and just plain fun he narrates herein takes place. It's where he birthed this book and industrialization birthed The Gilded Age, The Gay Nineties, and The Ages of Mass Entertainment, Consumerism, and Hysterics

Appendix 3

Interesting Tidbits of Baseball Lore

According to one source, professional baseball games were first played in 1869, and, initially, owners attempted to restrict attendance to the upper classes. The owners soon realized that ignoring the short-sleeved fans—the beer-drinking riffraff who made the game the national sport—would be an economic disaster and broadened their advertising and dropped the prices of tickets, hot dogs, beer, and souvenirs.

In 1867 Henry Chadwick accompanied the National Base Ball Club of Washington, D.C., on their inaugural national tour, as their official scorer. The next year, Chadwick wrote the first hardcover baseball book, *The Game of Base Ball*.

In 1874, Chadwick was instrumental in organizing a tour of England which included games of both baseball and cricket. In his role as journalist, he campaigned against the detrimental effects on the game of both alcohol and gambling.

Early baseball's 'bound rule' stipulated that if a fielder caught a batted ball on one bounce it would be recorded as an out. Chadwick was outspoken against the rule for many years, stating that fielders must catch a ball on the fly for it to be an out. In 1864, because of his efforts, the bound rule was eliminated for balls hit into fair territory. The bound rule for foul balls persisted into the 1880s.

Chadwick edited *The Beadle Dime Base-Ball Player*, the first annual baseball guide on public sale, as well as the *Spalding and Reach*

Annual Guide for several years. In this capacity, he promoted the game and influenced the infant discipline of sports journalism.

Appendix 4

More About Nellie Bly,

Aka Elizabeth Jane Cochran (May 5, 1864-January 27, 1922). In January 1885 the Pittsburg (then spelled without the 'h') Dispatch published a letter from 'Anxious Father,' who wondered what he should do with his five unmarried daughters, aged 18 to 26. Columnist Erasmus Wilson, who wrote as The Quiet Observer, responded with a misogynistic screed about working women, calling them 'a monstrosity' and insisting that their activities be centered in the home.

An outraged Cochran crafted a passionate rebuttal that grabbed the attention of editor George Madden, who offered her a job.

Madden then informed Cochran that she would need a pen name. equant practice for the few female reporters of the era. Inspiration struck when a clerk strolled past whistling 'Nellie Bly', a popular tune composed by Pittsburgh-born songwriter Stephen Foster.

Cochran rebelled when her writing assignments were confined to fashion, society functions, and flower shows. She yearned to tackle weightier issues, 'to do something no girl has done before.'

Bly did just that. She traveled to Mexico and wrote about government corruption; posed as an indigent mother to expose a black market baby-selling ring; addressed gender inequality embedded in divorce laws; posed as a sweatshop worker to expose abysmal conditions faced by women; and, in a journalistic feat of creativity and daring, feigned insanity to report on the deplorable conditions at Blackwell's Island in New York City, home to the infamous Women's Lunatic Asylum.

She made her own way, without help from anybody. She conceived and wrote the stories that she wanted to write and would improve the human condition.

Bly worked a little more than two years at the Dispatch.

Appendix 5

A Glance at Contemporary Jargon

- *Too high for his nut*: beyond someone's reach

- *Bottom fact*: The nut of the issue

- *Chicagoed*: Beaten soundly

- *See the elephant*: Visit all the sights of a town, especially the seedier ones

- *How come you so*: Staggering about in the presence of a shocked woman

- *Lally-cooler*: A real success

- *Shinning around*: Moving about quickly

- *Shoddyocracy*: Get rich selling shoddy merchandise

- *Some pumpkins*: A big deal

- *Like Thompson's colt*: Doing something unnecessarily

- *Tell a thumper*: Construct a clever lie

- *Wake snakes*: Get into mischief

APPENDIX 6

The Perilous Lines of Umpires

An umpire sounds off about his job:

"You see, I don't let these people (players) bother me in the least, . . . If a man takes these ballplayers seriously it is only a matter of a noticeably short time until they drive him to drink or to a madhouse"

"The epithet (a player) used was too much to be endured, even by an umpire. The crowd kept jeering me, but I paid no attention until a heavy beer mug struck me on the foot. I turned in time to see another coming. I picked up the first one and threw it underhanded into the crowd. I did not throw it at any person. . . I lost my temper, and this is the result." The "result" was that a fan was hospitalized with severe head injuries.

"Now you're getting a bit chesty, I see you've made a couple of good stops, knocked out a couple of hits and you think you're solid with the crowd. Well, I'll just tell you something. I'll give you the key to my room at the hotel, where everything is nice and quiet, and when we get in there alone, I'll break that jaw of yours so you can't kick for the rest of the season. I'll see that you get out quietly so you can explain your injury by saying you fell down somewhere.'"

"Players of XXX's stripe are fast making the game one that only a prize fighter or a thug has any business in."
A player defended his attack on an umpire: "I want to tell you one thing, that all with Irish blood in their veins will never stand being openly assaulted without retaliating."

A league executive remarked: "Altogether I am very badly off for umpires and don't know where to look for recruits,"

When an umpire forfeited a game to New York and fined Pittsburgh's Dick Padden, Frank Killian, and Pat Donovan $25 each, the Pirates kicked out the dressing-room windows. Later, the umpire punched a player.

In Pittsburgh, a mob "grossly insulted" an umpire, who then knocked down one fan, precipitating a general row, and fifteen police escorted him out. A block away a man hit an umpire in the back of his head.

Pete's other books include:

Speculative Dramas/Animal Compassion

1. The Rise and Fall of George Ferris, with Jeff Geissler, designer: America's most famous but invisible engineer still lives in his wheels around the world.

2. Who Murdered Topsy? Tom Edison was a great inventor and a cruel, selfish executioner

3. Who Murdered Mary? The town of Erwin, Tennessee hanged an innocent elephant

4. Who Murdered Jumbo? Did P. T. Barnum murder his circus's biggest attraction?

5. Elephants are Human Too: A collection of the above three books On happiness

6. The Power of Ethics, with Bill O'Rourke: the many tangible benefits of doing the right thing

7. The Power of Dignity: The Golden Rule in the real world

8. Divorce can be Such Sweet Sorrow: How to avoid the misery, angst and financial upsets of splitting up

9. An Accidental Life: autobiographical collection of serendipitous events and writings

On Financial And Social Success

1. The Power of Being Articulate: Your words can make you rich or poor

2. The Power of Writing Well: crafting clear, concise documents has never been more important or easier

3. The Little Black Book for Entrepreneurs: Lessons learned from a dedicated risk-taker

4. If You're so Smart, Why Aren't You Rich? Think rich, be rich; think poor, be poor

On Leadership

1. Your Character Can Make or Break Your Life: The importance of integrity and other traits that influence success

2. Hugging a Cloud: profits and meaning from the human side of business Are people really your most important asset?

3. The Beanstalk Jackpots: Lessons for climbing the ladder of success and finding the pot of gold

4. Leadership for Profitable Sustainability: Collection of writings about ethics and dignity

5. Sprinting from Good to Great: Collection of insightful essays and blogs

6. The Little Black Book of Human Resources Management, by

Barry Wolfe: A practical guide that is popular globally

On living well/autobiography

1. An Accidental life: Stories and commentary of a fortunate man

2. Shallow Water Sailor, by Ray Garra: Autobiography of a hectic and dangerous life in the Coast Guard

3. Peach, by Jenevieve Woods: Autobiography of a woman and her parents living with a debilitating disease

4. My Poems are Yours, by Jenevieve Woods: a heartfelt extension of Peach

5. Play Your Way, by Jenevieve Woods: A children's book with a call for compassion

6. Mushrooms for Dinner, by Brigitta Day: A German girl survives World War Two

On Financial And Social Success

1. The Power of Being Articulate: Your words can make you rich or poor

2. The Power of Writing Well: crafting clear, concise documents has never been more important or easier

3. The Little Black Book for Entrepreneurs: Lessons learned from a dedicated risk-taker

4. If You're so Smart, Why Aren't You Rich? Think rich, be rich; think poor, be poor

On Leadership

1. Your Character Can Make or Break Your Life: The importance of integrity and other traits that influence success

2. Hugging a Cloud: profits and meaning from the human side of business Are people really your most important asset?

3. The Beanstalk Jackpots: Lessons for climbing the ladder of success and finding the pot of gold

4. Leadership for Profitable Sustainability: Collection of writings about ethics and dignity

5. Sprinting from Good to Great: Collection of insightful essays and blogs

6. The Little Black Book of Human Resources Management, by

Barry Wolfe: A practical guide that is popular globally

On living well/autobiography

1. An Accidental life: Stories and commentary of a fortunate man

2. Shallow Water Sailor, by Ray Garra: Autobiography of a hectic and dangerous life in the Coast Guard

3. Peach, by Jenevieve Woods: Autobiography of a woman and her parents living with a debilitating disease

4. My Poems are Yours, by Jenevieve Woods: a heartfelt extension of Peach

5. Play Your Way, by Jenevieve Woods: A children's book with a call for compassion

6. Mushrooms for Dinner, by Brigitta Day: A German girl survives World War Two

On Fun And Games

1. Rockin' Romance, by Dante Lorenzo Valentino, Ph.D. A raunchy romp through bizarre sexual exploits and relationships

2. BigShots' Bull*!@#: Essays and commentary on commerce, politics, and life

For more: theexpressivepress.org

www.ingramcontent.com/pod-product-compliance
Lightning Source LLC
La Vergne TN
LVHW012026060526
838201LV00061B/4484